I0628760

WITHDRAWN

The
Outbreak of
the Civil War

Other books in the At Issue in History series:

The
Outbreak of
the Civil War

Jean Alicia Elster, *Book Editor*

Daniel Leone, *President*
Bonnie Szumski, *Publisher*
Scott Barbour, *Managing Editor*

 **AT ISSUE IN HISTORY**

GREENHAVEN
PRESS®

San Diego • Detroit • New York • San Francisco • Cleveland
New Haven, Conn. • Waterville, Maine • London • Munich

THOMSON
━━━━━✳━━━━━ ™
GALE

LIBRARY OF CONGRESS CATALOGING-IN-PUBLICATION DATA

The outbreak of the Civil War / Jean Alicia Elster, book editor.
    p. cm. — (At issue in history)
    Includes bibliographical references and index.
    ISBN 0-7377-1344-5 (lib. bdg. : alk. paper) —
    ISBN 0-7377-1345-3 (pbk. : alk. paper)
    1. United States—History—Civil War, 1861–1865—Causes. 2. Slavery—Political aspects—United States—History—19th century. 3. Secession—Southern States. 4. United States—History—Civil War, 1861–1865—Causes—Sources. 5. Slavery—Political aspects—United States—History—19th century—Sources. 6. Secession—Southern States—Sources. I. Elster, Jean Alicia. II. Series.
E458 .O88 2003
973.7'11—dc21   2002042610

Printed in the United States of America

Contents

an evil—a threat to the Union—and proposed
that the new territories be free of the presence of
slaves.

Chapter 2: The Secession Crisis

Chapter 3: The Causes and Consequences of the Civil War

to the North. He explains that this transformation cemented the Northern vision of the country as an industrial capitalist nation.

C. Vann Woodward describes the shift in race relations following the war: The physical oppression of slavery gave way to a brief period of relatively egalitarian relations, which was soon followed by systematic discrimination and legalized segregation under Jim Crow.

Foreword

Historian Robert Weiss defines history simply as "a record and interpretation of past events." Both elements—record and interpretation—are necessary, Weiss argues.

> Names, dates, places, and events are the essence of history. But historical writing is not a compendium of facts. It consists of facts placed in a sequence to tell a connected story. A work of history is not merely a story, however. It also must analyze what happened and *why*—that is, it must interpret the past for the reader.

For example, the events of December 7, 1941, that led President Franklin D. Roosevelt to call it "a date which will live in infamy" are fairly well known and straightforward. A force of Japanese planes and submarines launched a torpedo and bombing attack on American military targets in Pearl Harbor, Hawaii. The surprise assault sank five battleships, disabled or sank fourteen additional ships, and left almost twenty-four hundred American soldiers and sailors dead. On the following day, the United States formally entered World War II when Congress declared war on Japan.

These facts and consequences were almost immediately communicated to the American people who heard reports about Pearl Harbor and President Roosevelt's response on the radio. All realized that this was an important and pivotal event in American and world history. Yet the news from Pearl Harbor raised many unanswered questions. Why did Japan decide to launch such an offensive? Why were the attackers so successful in catching America by surprise? What did the attack reveal about the two nations, their people, and their leadership? What were its causes, and what were its effects? Political leaders, academic historians, and students look to learn the basic facts of historical events and to read the intepretations of these events by many different sources, both primary and secondary, in order to develop a more complete picture of the event in a historical context.

In the case of Pearl Harbor, several important questions surrounding the event remain in dispute, most notably the role of President Roosevelt. Some historians have blamed his policies for deliberately provoking Japan to attack in order to propel America into World War II; a few have gone so far as to accuse him of knowing of the impending attack but not informing others. Other historians, examining the same event, have exonerated the president of such charges, arguing that the historical evidence does not support such a theory.

The Greenhaven At Issue in History series recognizes that many important historical events have been interpreted differently and in some cases remain shrouded in controversy. Each volume features a collection of articles that focus on a topic that has sparked controversy among eyewitnesses, contemporary observers, and historians. An introductory essay sets the stage for each topic by presenting background and context. Several chapters then examine different facets of the subject at hand with readings chosen for their diversity of opinion. Each selection is preceded by a summary of the author's main points and conclusions. A bibliography is included for those students interested in pursuing further research. An annotated table of contents and thorough index help readers to quickly locate material of interest. Taken together, the contents of each of the volumes in the Greenhaven At Issue in History series will help students become more discriminating and thoughtful readers of history.

Introduction

The ten years preceding the outbreak of the U.S. Civil War in 1861 were some of the most tumultuous and chaotic years in American history. During this turbulent decade, the nation's stability faltered as its citizens sought to address issues fundamental to its continued existence and to its evolving way of life. These issues centered around, or were affected by, the debate over slavery. The conflict over slavery was at the heart of the regional differences between the North and the South. In addition, Americans were sharply divided over questions such as the morality of slavery, the right of states to determine for themselves whether slavery would be allowed within their borders, the possible expansion of slavery into the western territories, and whether Southern states should be allowed to secede from the Union in order to maintain slavery. Ultimately, the failure to resolve this conflict over slavery culminated in the outbreak of the Civil War.

Regional Differences

Early in the nation's history, the geography of the North and South led states along two separate paths of economic development. Within the South, according to historian William C. Davis, "soil and climate lent themselves chiefly to large-scale agriculture and the planting of cash crops, first tobacco and then cotton."[1] Slavery was an essential part of this agrarian economic system because it produced a steady supply of cheap labor. This labor, in turn, allowed landowners to expand their holdings and maintain profits. On the other hand, the situation in the North was quite different. An abundance of natural resources, along with a large influx of European immigrants, ensured that the North would experience phenomenal industrial growth with a labor pool eager to fill an ever-increasing demand for workers.

The tension that mounted between the different needs of these two competing economic systems was not based on a consideration of the morality of slavery. Rather, the regional differences focused on the question of which system would dominate the future economic development of the country—the free labor of the industrial North or the slave labor of the agrarian South. A major conflict, on this issue alone, was unavoidable.

The Morality of Slavery

Simultaneous to the debate over differing economic systems, the question of the morality of slavery emerged as an issue in its own right with the rise of the abolitionist movement. This movement, which viewed the enslavement of blacks as an evil, began in the early 1830s. However, the antislavery movement grew dramatically, particularly with whites in the North, after the passage of the Fugitive Slave Law in 1850. This law, which drastically expanded federal participation in capturing runaway slaves and returning them to their owners, only served to intensify the debate over slavery. Abolitionists were appalled that the federal government would give support to the institution of slavery by further aiding in the ability of slaveholders to reclaim their human chattel. According to the Civil War Society, this law, which was created to "quell regional tensions over the slavery issue . . . had precisely the opposite effect, inflaming passions in both the North and South, which contributed enormously to the country's ominous movement toward disunion."[2]

States' Rights and Popular Sovereignty

While antislavery sentiments were voiced through the abolitionist movement, the proslavery movement expressed itself through the Southern notion of "states' rights." The concept of states' rights and the relative power of the states in relation to the federal government had become controversial issues soon after the adoption of the U.S. Constitution in 1787. However, the definition of the term took on a much more narrow meaning in the early nineteenth century. "Starting in the 1820s . . . the states' rights argument centered more and more upon the practice of slavery."[3] The Southern states sought to protect their agrarian way of life by retaining the right to choose to keep, or not to keep, the institution of slavery within their borders without federal intervention.

The issue of slavery was not limited to the conflict between the Southern and Northern states. As the country expanded to the west, the slavery question traveled with it. Illinois senator Stephen A. Douglas introduced the Kansas-Nebraska Act in 1854 in order to address this question. Douglas proposed dividing the remaining territory of the Louisiana Purchase (land from the Mississippi River west to the Rocky Mountains and from the Gulf of Mexico north to Canada) into the territories of Kansas and Nebraska. To settle the question of whether slavery would be allowed in this area, he promoted the concept of popular sovereignty.

The premise behind popular sovereignty seemed simple—the people residing in the territories had the right to decide whether slavery would be allowed to exist there. However, Douglas, who had declared himself neutral on the question of slavery, had not anticipated the furor that would erupt among various groups over the possibility that slavery might be introduced in areas of the country where it previously did not exist. As stated by historian David M. Potter, "Instead of settling a controversy, the adoption of the act transplanted the controversy . . . to the plains of Kansas."[4] The phrase "bleeding Kansas" entered the American political vocabulary as a result of violent battles between antislavery and proslavery forces during this era. The question of slavery in the territories thus became one of the issues that drew the United States into the Civil War.

Secession and the Outbreak of the Civil War

When the Southern states felt that the interests of the Union not only favored the industrial North but also were likely to intrude on their right to maintain a system of slavery, they threatened to secede. Many Southerners believed that secession might be the only way they could protect their sovereign rights and maintain the institution of slavery. This talk of secession led to a debate over whether any state had the right to secede. Most citizens living in the North did not believe the South had a right to secede. In addition, some Southerners, such as Senator Andrew Johnson, continued to believe in the Union and argued that any disagreements with the federal government over issues such as slavery should be handled within the framework of the Constitution. Yet, as secession of one or more of the Southern states seemed inevitable, the

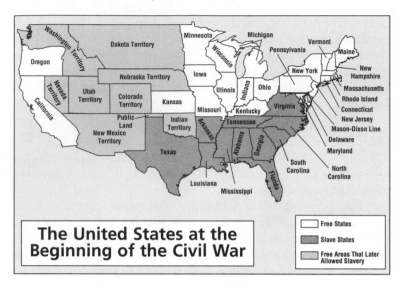

The United States at the Beginning of the Civil War

Free States

Slave States

Free Areas That Later Allowed Slavery

question became, how should the federal government respond to such a move?

Lincoln's election as the sixteenth president of the United States in 1860 proved to be too much for the slave states of the South. On December 20, 1860, South Carolina was the first state to secede from the Union. That act of secession was the culmination of years of struggle within the Southern slaveholding states to balance their loyalty to the Union with their fierce allegiance to a uniquely Southern way of life. Once South Carolina seceded, ten more Southern states eventually followed, forming the Confederate States of America.

By the time Lincoln was sworn in, war between the Northern and Southern states loomed. In his inaugural address on March 4, 1861, Lincoln pledged to uphold the Union. He also pledged that there would be "no invasion or using of force" against the citizens of the Union. Yet, other politicians were already determined to exercise force to bring any states that chose to secede back into the Union.

As one of its first official acts, the Confederate government sought to confiscate federal property located in the South, including Fort Sumter. On April 12, 1861, the Confederates opened fire on the fort, and it soon fell into Confederate hands. President Lincoln's response was to call for seventy-five thousand volunteer soldiers. The nation's fate was sealed for what would be four more years of battles.

The Outcome of the Civil War

A Confederate surrender at Appomattox Courthouse on April 12, 1865, marked the end of the Civil War. By the war's end, more lives had been lost than in any war in U.S. history; that fact remains true to this day. Over 350,000 Union soldiers and approximately 245,000 Confederate soldiers died of battlefield wounds or disease. Another 30,000 died of other causes related to the war.

One of the most dramatic outcomes of the war involved the institution of slavery. While the Emancipation Proclamation, issued on New Year's Day 1863 by President Abraham Lincoln, freed all slaves living in the South, the Thirteenth Amendment, ratified in 1865, ended slavery existing anywhere in the United States. Also, the defeat of the South required the very deliberate process of reuniting the Confederate states with the Union. This period, called Reconstruction, was the North's attempt to help rebuild the South by providing economic relief, establishing a public school system, and giving blacks the right to vote and have a voice in the political system. Many of these advancements were severely restricted over time. Yet they initially laid the groundwork for the reunification of the states and provided a small measure of healing for the nation.

Notes

1. William C. Davis, *A Concise History of the Civil War.* Conshohocken, PA: Eastern National, 1994, p. 1.
2. Civil War Society, *Encyclopedia of the Civil War.* New York: Portland House, 1997, p. 139.
3. Civil War Society, *Encyclopedia of the Civil War*, p. 346.
4. David M. Potter, *The Impending Crisis: 1848–1861.* New York: Harper Torchbooks, 1976, p. 199.

Chapter **1**

The Growing Conflict over Slavery

1

An Undivided Union Can Bring an End to Slavery

Frederick Douglass

All abolitionist groups were adamant in their insistence on an end to slavery in the United States. However, these groups advocated different means to achieve that goal. Some wanted only to stop the expansion of slavery into the territories. Others favored a system of "colonization" in which free blacks would be sent to Africa. Still others advocated violent means to rid the country of the evil of slavery. Frederick Douglass, a former slave who escaped by posing as a free black sailor and rose to become one of the most famous abolitionists in U.S. history, espoused another ideology. He believed that the U.S. Constitution was an antislavery document, and he opposed the dissolution of the Union as a means of ridding the country of the institution of slavery. The following selection, first published in the June 8, 1849 edition of the *Liberator*, was directed toward the American Anti-Slavery Society in response to its doctrine of "no union with slaveholders."

Its [the Constitution's] language is, "We the people"; not we the white people, not even we the citizens, not we the privileged class, not we the high, not we the low, but we the people; not we the horses, sheep, and swine, and wheelbarrows, but we the people, we the human inhabitants; and if Negroes are people, they are included in the benefits for which the Constitution of America was ordained and established. But how dare any man who pretends to be the friend

Frederick Douglass, "The Constitution, the Union, and Slavery," *The Liberator*, June 8, 1849.

to the Negro thus gratuitously concede away what the Negro has a right to claim under the Constitution? Why should such friends invent new arguments to increase the hopelessness of his bondage? This, I undertake to say, as the conclusion of the whole matter, that the constitutionality of slavery can be made out only by disregarding the plain and common-sense reading of the Constitution itself; by disregarding and casting away as worthless the most beneficent rules of legal interpretation; by ruling the Negro outside of these beneficent rules; by claiming everything for slavery; by denying everything for freedom; by assuming that the Constitution does not mean what it says, and that it says what it does not mean; by disregarding the written Constitution, and interpreting it in the light of a secret understanding. It is in this mean, contemptible, and underhand method that the American Constitution is pressed into the service of slavery. They go everywhere else for proof that the Constitution is pro-slavery but to the Constitution itself. The Constitution declares that no person shall be deprived of life, liberty, or property, without due process of law; it secures to every man the right of trial by jury, the privilege of the writ of *habeas corpus*—that great writ that put an end to slavery and slave-hunting in England; it secures to every State a republican form of government. Any one of these provisions in the hands of Abolition Statesmen, and backed up by a right moral sentiment, would put an end to slavery in America. . . .

But how dare any man who pretends to be the friend to the Negro thus gratuitously concede away what the Negro has a right to claim under the Constitution?

The way to abolish slavery in America is to vote such men into power, as will use their powers for the abolition of slavery.

Argument Against Dissolving the Union
. . . My argument against the dissolution of the American Union is this: It would place the slave system more exclusively under the control of the slaveholding States, and

withdraw it from the power in the Northern States which is opposed to slavery. Slavery is essentially barbarous in its character. It, above all things else, dreads the presence of an advanced civilization. It flourishes best where it meets no reproving frowns, and hears no condemning voices. While in the Union it will meet with both. Its hope of life in the last resort is to get out of the Union. I am, therefore, for drawing the bond of the Union more closely, and bringing the slave States more completely under the power of the free States. What they most dread, that I most desire. I have much confidence in the instincts of the slaveholders. They see, more-over, that if there is once a will in the people of America to abolish slavery, there is no word, no syllable in the Constitution to forbid the result. They see that the Constitution has not saved slavery in Rhode Island, in Connecticut, in New York, or Pennsylvania; that the free States have increased from one to eighteen in number, while the slave States have only added

Frederick Douglass

three to their original number. There were twelve slave States at the beginning of the Government; there are fifteen now. There was one free State at the beginning of the Government: there are eighteen now. The dissolution of the Union would not give the North a single advantage over slavery, but would take from it many. Within the Union we have a firm basis of opposition to slavery. It is opposed to all the great objects of the Constitution. The dissolution of the Union is not only an unwise but a cowardly measure—fif-teen millions running away from three hundred and fifty thousand slaveholders. Mr. [William Lloyd] Garrison and his friends tell us that while in the Union we are responsible for slavery. He and they sing out "No union with slavehold-ers," and refuse to vote. I admit our responsibility for slav-ery while in the Union; but I deny that going out of the Union would free us from that responsibility. . . .

Disagreement with Other Abolitionists

Its [American Anti-Slavery Society] doctrine of "No union with slaveholders," carried out, dissolves the Union, and leaves the slaves and their masters to fight their own battles, in their own way. This I hold to be an abandonment of the great idea with which that Society started. It started to free the slave. It ends by leaving the slave to free himself. It started with the purpose to imbue the heart of the nation with sentiments favorable to the abolition of slavery, and ends, by seeking to free the North from all responsibility for slavery, other than if slavery were in Great Britain, or under some other nationality. This, I say, is the practical abandonment of the idea with which that Society started.

I am . . . for drawing the bond of the Union more closely, and bringing the slave States more completely under the power of the free States.

. . . But this is not the worse fault of this Society. Its chief energies are expended in confirming the opinion, that the United States Constitution is, and was, intended to be a slaveholding instrument—thus piling up, between the slave and his freedom, the huge work of the abolition of the Government, as an indispensable condition to Emancipation. My point here is, first, the Constitution is, according to its reading, an anti-slavery document; and, secondly, to dissolve the Union, as a means to abolish slavery, is about as wise as it would be to burn up this city, in order to get the thieves out of it. But again we hear the motto, "No union with slaveholders"; and I answer it, as that noble champion of liberty, Nathaniel P. Rogers [abolitionist leader], answered it with a more sensible motto, namely—"No union with slaveholding." I would unite with anybody to do right, and with nobody to do wrong. And as the Union, under the Constitution, requires me to do nothing which is wrong, and gives me many facilities for doing good, I cannot go with the American Anti-Slavery Society in its doctrine of disunion.

2

Only the Dissolution of the Union Can End Slavery

William Lloyd Garrison

The American Anti-Slavery Society was one of the country's foremost organizations in the abolition movement. It promoted an immediate, rather than piecemeal, approach to the end of slavery and total access for blacks to the political system. One of this group's founders, William Lloyd Garrison, was so closely identified with the abolitionist movement that his name became almost synonymous with it. His leadership within the antislavery movement and his strong viewpoints on the Constitution and the Union garnered him as many detractors as they did supporters. The following article displays his strong feelings against slavery, explains his belief that the U.S. Constitution actually supports slavery, and promotes his viewpoint that the dissolution of the Union is the only means to effectively end slavery.

There are some very worthy men, who are gravely trying to convince this slaveholding and slave-trading nation, that it has an Anti-Slavery Constitution, if it did but know it—always has had it since it was a nation—and so designed it to be from the beginning! Hence, all slaveholding under it is illegal, and ought in virtue of it to be forthwith abolished by act of Congress. As rationally attempt to convince the American people that they inhabit the moon, and

William Lloyd Garrison, *Selections from the Writings and Speeches of William Lloyd Garrison*. Westport, CT: Negro Universities Press, 1968.

'run upon all fours,' as that they have not intelligently, deliberately and purposely entered into a covenant, by which three millions of slaves are now held securely in bondage! They are not to be let off so easily, either by indignant Heaven or outraged Earth! To tell them that, for three score years, they have misunderstood and misinterpreted their own Constitution, in a manner gross and distorted beyond any thing known in human history; that Washington, Jefferson, Adams, all who framed that Constitution—the Supreme Court of the United States, and all its branches, and all other Courts—the national Congress and all State Legislatures—have utterly perverted its scope and meaning—is the coolest and absurdest thing ever heard of beneath the stars! No, not thus are they to be allowed to escape hot censure and unsparing condemnation. They have committed no blunder; they have not erred through stupidity; they have not been misled by any legal sophistry. They are verily guilty of the most atrocious crimes, and have sinned against the clearest light ever vouchsafed to any people. They have designedly 'framed mischief by a law,' and consigned to chains and infamy an inoffensive and helpless race. Hence, it is not an error in legal interpretation that they are to correct, but they are to be arraigned as criminals of the deepest dye, warned of the wrath to come, and urged to the immediate confession and abandonment of this great 'besetting sin.' 'Now, therefore, go to, speak to the men of Judah, and to the inhabitants of Jerusalem, saying, Thus saith the Lord, Behold, I frame evil against you, and devise a device against you; return ye now every one from his evil way, and make your ways and your doings good.'

And is any one so infatuated as to believe, that what could not be done sixty years ago, with only six hundred thousand slaves to be liberated, without convulsing the country, can now be done 'by the strict rules of legal interpretation'?

Some are unwilling to admit the possibility of legalizing slavery, because of its foul and monstrous character. But what iniquity may not men commit by agreement? and what obligations so diabolical, that men may not promise to perform them to the letter? To say that men have no right to do wrong is a truism; to intimate that they have not the power to do so is an absurdity. If they have the power, it is possible for them to use it; and no where do they use it with more alacrity, or on a more gigantic scale, than in the United States.

The Meaning of the Constitution

'To ascertain the meaning of the Constitution,' we are told, 'we are to subject it, as we do any other law, to the strict rules of legal interpretation.' It seems to us that this statement is extremely fallacious. The Constitution is not a statute, but a UNION, A COMPACT formed between separate and independent colonies, with conflicting interests and diverse sentiments, to be reconciled in the best manner possible, by concession and compromise, for the attainment of a common object—their own safety and welfare against a common enemy. What those concessions and compromises were, all knew when the compact was framed and adopted; they related to the prosecution of the foreign slave trade for twenty years, to the allowance of a slave representation in Congress, to the hunting of fugitive slaves, and to the suppression of domestic insurrections, for the special benefit of the slave States; and to direct taxation and the navigation laws, in behalf of the free States. The Constitution of the United States, then, is a form of government, having special powers and prerogatives of its own—created under great emergencies and with peculiar features—unlike any thing in ancient or modern times; a form of government, we reiterate, not a legislative enactment, but under which, and by authority of which, laws are to be passed, but never to be interpreted to the subversion of the government, or by a higher standard! . . .

And is any one so infatuated as to believe, that what could not be done sixty years ago, with only six hundred thousand slaves to be liberated, without convulsing the country, can now be done 'by the strict rules of legal interpretation,' in utter disregard of all the facts and all the precedents in our national history, with fifteen instead of six slave States, and three millions of slaves, without filling the land with a deluge of blood? Supposing—what is not within the scope of probabilities—that we could win over to their view of the Constitution a majority, ay, the entire body of the people of the North, so that they could control the action of Congress through their representatives, and in this manner decree the abolition of slavery throughout the South—could we hope to witness even the enactment of such a decree, (to say nothing of its enforcement,) without its being accompanied by the most fearful consequences? Does any reply, that a fear of consequences should not deter us from doing right? This is cheerfully granted: but are these Anti-Slavery interpreters ready for a civil war, as the inevitable result of their construction of the Constitution? What reason have they to believe, from the past, that a civil war would not immediately follow, in the case supposed? . . .

Let us, who profess to abhor slavery, and who claim to be freemen indeed, dissolve the bands that connect us with the Slave Power, religiously and politically.

Where, then, and what is to be the Union, under this new constitutional interpretation?

Call to Action

Away with all verbal casuistry, all legal quibbling, the idle parade of Lord Mansfield's decision in the case of Somerset, the useless appeals to Blackstone's Commentaries, and the like, to prove that the United States Constitution is an Anti-Slavery instrument! It is worse than labor lost, and, as a false issue, cannot advance, but must rather retard, the Anti-Slavery movement. Let there be no dodging, no shuffling, no evasion. Let us confess the sin of our fathers, and our own sin as a people, in conspiring for the degradation and enslavement of the colored race among us. Let us be honest with the facts of history, and acknowledge the compromises that were made to secure the adoption of the Constitution, and the consequent establishment of the Union. Let us, who profess to abhor slavery, and who claim to be freemen indeed, dissolve the bands that connect us with the Slave Power, religiously and politically; not doubting that a faithful adherence to principle will be the wisest policy, the highest expediency, for ourselves and our posterity, for the miserable victims of Southern oppression, and for the cause of liberty throughout the world.

We regard this as indeed a solemn crisis, which requires of every man sobriety of thought, prophetic forecast, independent judgment, invincible determination, and a sound heart. A revolutionary step is one that should not be taken hastily, nor followed under the influence of impulsive imitation. To know what spirits they are of—whether they have counted the cost of the warfare—what are the principles they advocate—and how they are to achieve their object—is the first duty of revolutionists.

But, while circumspection and prudence are excellent qualities in every great emergency, they become the allies of tyranny whenever they restrain prompt, bold and decisive action against it.

Charges Against the Constitution

We charge upon the present national compact, that it was formed at the expense of human liberty, by a profligate surrender of principle, and to this hour is cemented with human blood.

We charge upon the American Constitution, that it contains provisions, and enjoins duties, which make it unlawful for freemen to take the oath of allegiance to it, because they are expressly designed to favor a slaveholding oligarchy, and, consequently, to make one portion of the people a prey to another.

A partnership between right and wrong is wholly wrong.

It was pleaded at the time of its adoption, it is pleaded now, that, without such a compromise, there could have been no union; that, without union, the colonies would have become an easy prey to the mother country; and, hence, that it was an act of necessity, deplorable indeed when viewed alone, but absolutely indispensable to the safety of the republic.

To this we reply: The plea is as profligate as the act was tyrannical. It is the jesuitical doctrine, that the end sanctifies the means. It is a confession of sin, but the denial of any guilt in its perpetration. This plea is sufficiently broad to cover all the oppression and villany that the sun has witnessed in his circuit, since God said, 'Let there be light.' It assumes that to be practicable which is impossible, namely, that there can be freedom with slavery, union with injustice, and safety with bloodguiltiness. A union of virtue with pollution is the triumph of licentiousness. A partnership between right and wrong is wholly wrong. A compromise of the principles of justice is the deification of crime.

No one can innocently swear to support the Constitution.

Better that the American Union had never been formed, than that it should have been obtained at such a frightful cost! If they were guilty who fashioned it, but who could not foresee all its frightful consequences, how much more guilty are they, who, in full view of all that has resulted from it, clamor for its perpetuity! If it was sinful at the commencement to adopt it, on the ground of escaping a greater evil, is it not equally sinful to swear to support it for the same reason, or until, in process of time, it be purged from its corruption?

The fact is, the compromise alluded to, instead of effecting a union, rendered it impracticable; unless by the

Abolitionist groups, such as the American Anti-Slavery Society, insisted on an end to all slavery in the United States.

term union we are to understand the absolute reign of the slaveholding power over the whole country, to the prostration of Northern rights. It is not certain, it is not even probable, that if the present Constitution had not been adopted, the mother country would have reconquered the colonies. The spirit that would have chosen danger in preference to crime, to perish with justice rather than live with dishonor, to dare and suffer whatever might betide, rather than sacrifice the rights of one human being, could never have been subjugated by any mortal power. Surely, it is paying a poor tribute to the valor and devotion of our revolutionary fathers in the cause of liberty, to say that, if they had sternly refused to sacrifice their principles, they would have fallen an easy prey to the despotic power of England.

It is absurd, it is false, it is an insult to the common sense of mankind, to pretend that the Constitution was intended to embrace the entire population of the country.

To the argument, that the words 'slaves' and 'slavery' are not to be found in the Constitution, and therefore that it was never intended to give any protection or countenance to the slave system, it is sufficient to reply, that though no such words are contained in the instrument, other words were used, intelligently and specifically, to meet the necessities of slavery; and that these were adopted in good faith, to be observed until a constitutional change could be effected. On this point, as to the design of certain provisions, no intelligent man can honestly entertain a doubt. If it be objected, that though these provisions were meant to cover slavery, yet, as they can fairly be interpreted to mean something exactly the reverse, it is allowable to give to them such an interpretation, especially as the cause of freedom will thereby be promoted—we reply, that this is to advocate fraud and violence toward one of the contracting parties, whose cooperation was secured only by an express agreement and understanding between them both, in regard to the clauses alluded to; and that such a construction, if enforced by pains and penalties, would unquestionably lead to a civil war, in which the aggrieved party would justly claim to have been betrayed, and robbed of their constitutional rights.

Again, if it be said, that those clauses, being immoral, are null and void—we reply, it is true they are not to be observed; but it is also true, that they are portions of an instrument, the support of which, as a whole, is required by oath or affirmation; and, therefore, because they are immoral, and because of this obligation to enforce immorality, no one can innocently swear to support the Constitution.

Constitutional Interpretation

Again, if it be objected, that the Constitution was formed by the people of the United States, in order to establish justice, to promote the general welfare, and secure the blessings of liberty to themselves and their posterity; and, therefore, it is to be so construed as to harmonize with these objects; we reply, again, that its language is not to be interpreted in a sense which neither of the contracting parties understood, and which would frustrate every design of their alliance—to wit, union at the expense of the colored population of the country. Moreover, nothing is more certain than that the preamble alluded to never included, in the minds of those who framed it, those who were then pining in bondage—for, in that case, a general emancipation of the slaves would have instantly been proclaimed throughout the United States. The words, 'secure the blessings of liberty to ourselves and our posterity,' assuredly did not mean to include the slave population. 'To promote the general welfare,' referred to their own welfare exclusively. 'To establish justice,' was understood to be for their sole benefit as slaveholders, and the guilty abettors of slavery. This is demonstrated by other parts of the same instrument, and by their own practice under it.

We rise in rebellion against a despotism incomparably more dreadful than that which induced the colonists to take up arms against the mother country.

We would not detract aught from what is justly their due; but it is as reprehensible to give them credit for what they did not possess, as it is to rob them of what is theirs. It is absurd, it is false, it is an insult to the common sense of mankind, to pretend that the Constitution was intended to embrace the entire population of the country under its sheltering wings; or that the parties to it were actuated by a sense of justice and the spirit of impartial liberty; or that it needs no alteration, but only a new interpretation, to make it harmonize with the object aimed at by its adoption. As truly might it be argued, that because it is asserted in the Declaration of Independence, that all men are created equal, and endowed with an inalienable right to liberty, therefore none of its signers were slaveholders, and since its adoption slavery has been banished from the American soil! The truth is, our fathers were intent on securing liberty to themselves, without being very scrupulous as to the means they used to accomplish their purpose. They were not actuated by the spirit of universal philanthropy; and though in words they recognised occasionally the brotherhood of the human race, in practice they continually denied it. They did not blush to enslave a portion of their fellow-men, and to buy and sell them as cattle in the market, while they were fighting against the oppression of the mother country, and boasting of their regard for the rights of man. Why, then, concede to them virtues which they did not possess? Why cling to the falsehood, that they were no respecters of persons in the formation of the government? . . .

Constitution Is Powerless

If, in utter disregard of all historical facts, it is still asserted, that the Constitution needs no amendment to make it a free instrument, adapted to all the exigencies of a free people, and was never intended to give any strength or countenance to the slave system—the indignant spirit of insulted Liberty replies:—'What though the assertion be true? Of what avail is a mere piece of parchment? In itself, though it be written all over with words of truth and freedom—though its provisions be as impartial and just as words can express, or the imagination paint—though it be as pure as the gospel, and breathe only the spirit of Heaven—it is powerless; it has no executive vitality; it is a lifeless corpse, even though beautiful in death. I am famishing for lack of bread! How is my appetite relieved by holding up to my gaze a painted loaf? I am manacled, wounded, bleeding, dying! What consolation is it to know, that they who are seeking to destroy my life, profess in words to be my friends? If the liberties of the people have been betrayed—if judgment has been turned away backward, and justice standeth afar off, and truth has fallen in the streets, and equity cannot enter—if the princes of the land are roaring lions, the judges evening wolves, the people light and treacherous persons, the priests covered with pollution—if we are living under a frightful despotism, which scoffs at all constitutional restraints, and wields the resources of the nation to promote its own bloody purposes— tell us not that the forms of freedom are still left to us! 'Would such tameness and submission have freighted the May Flower for Plymouth Rock? Would it have resisted the Stamp Act, the Tea Tax, or any of those entering wedges of tyranny with which the British government sought to rive the liberties of America? The wheel of the Revolution would have rusted on its axle, if a spirit so weak had been the only power to give it motion. Did our fathers say, when their rights and liberties were infringed—"Why, what is done cannot be undone! That is the first thought!" No, it was the last thing they thought of: or, rather, it never entered their minds at all. They sprang to the conclusion at once—"What is done shall be undone! That is our first and only thought!"'. . .

The Constitution which subjects them to hopeless bondage is one that we cannot swear to support.

It is of little consequence who is on the throne, if there be behind it a power mightier than the throne. It matters not what is the theory of the government, if the practice of the government be unjust and tyrannical. We rise in rebellion against a despotism incomparably more dreadful than that which induced the colonists to take up arms against the mother country; not on account of a three-penny tax on tea, but because fetters of living iron are fastened on the limbs of millions of our countrymen, and our most sacred rights are trampled in the dust. As citizens of the State, we appeal to the State in vain for protection and redress. As citizens of the United States, we are treated as outlaws in one half of the country, and the national government consents to our destruction. We are denied the right of locomotion, freedom of speech, the right of petition, the liberty of the press, the right peaceably to assemble together to protest against oppression and plead for liberty—at least, in fifteen States of the Union. If we venture, as avowed and unflinching abolitionists, to travel South of Mason and Dixon's line, we do so at the peril of our lives. If we would escape torture and death, on visiting any of the slave States, we must stifle our conscientious convictions, bear no testimony against cruelty and tyranny, suppress the struggling emotions of humanity, divest ourselves of all letters and papers of an anti-slavery character, and do homage to the slaveholding power—or run the risk of a cruel martyrdom! These are appalling and undeniable facts.

No Union with Slaveholders

Three millions of the American people are crushed under the American Union! They are held as slaves, trafficked as merchandise, registered as goods and chattels! The government gives them no protection—the government is their enemy, the government keeps them in chains! Where they lie bleeding, we are prostrate by their side—in their sorrows and sufferings we participate—their stripes are inflicted on our bodies, their shackles are fastened on our limbs, their cause is ours! The Union which grinds them to the dust rests upon us, and with them we will struggle to overthrow it! The Constitution which subjects them to hopeless bondage is one that we cannot swear to support. Our motto is, 'No Union with Slaveholders,' either religious or political. They are the fiercest enemies of mankind, and the bitterest foes of God! We separate from them, not in anger, not in malice, not for a selfish purpose, not to do them an injury, not to cease warning, exhorting, reproving them for their crimes, not to leave the perishing bondman to his fate—O no! But to clear our skirts of innocent blood—to give the oppressor no countenance—and to hasten the downfall of slavery in America, and throughout the world! . . .

The form of government that shall succeed the present government of the United States, let time determine.

The form of government that shall succeed the present government of the United States, let time determine. It would be a waste of time to argue that question, until the people are regenerated and turned from their iniquity. Ours is no anarchical movement, but one of order and obedience. In ceasing from oppression, we establish liberty. What is now fragmentary shall in due time be crystalized, and shine like a gem set in the heavens, for a light to all coming ages.

3

Slavery Should Not End

George Fitzhugh

The battle between the Northern and the Southern way of life occurred long before the first shot was fired at Fort Sumter. A battle of words pitted Northern apologists for "free labor" (meaning, actually, paid labor) against Southern defenders of the slave system. Those latter defenders believed that the system of human slavery was not only the most economically equitable but also the most humane. Citing the squalid slums of the North as one example of the inhumanity of the industrial system, the pro-slavery argument took a paternalistic view of the Southern way of life: Slaves were fed and clothed from the cradle to the grave. There was no competition for jobs. Slaves knew their place as subservient members of society, and masters accepted their responsibilities for these charges. In return, masters not only received labor in their fields and homes but the time to maintain and cultivate a genteel, intellectually superior way of life. This Southern view is presented in the following excerpts from an 1850 pamphlet by George Fitzhugh, a Virginia lawyer, plantation owner, and intellectual.

L iberty and equality are new things under the sun. The free states of antiquity abounded with slaves. The feudal system that supplanted Roman institutions changed the form of slavery, but brought with it neither liberty nor equality. France and the Northern States of our Union have alone fully and fairly tried the experiment of a social organization founded upon universal liberty and equality of rights. England has only approximated to this condition in her commercial and manufacturing cities. The examples of

George Fitzhugh, "Sociology for The South," *Slavery Defended: The Views of the Old South*, edited by Eric L. McKitrick. Englewood Cliffs, NJ: Prentice-Hall, Inc., 1963.

small communities in Europe are not fit exponents of the working of the system. In France and in our Northern States the experiment has already failed, if we are to form our opinions from the discontent of the masses, or to believe the evidence of the Socialists, Communists, Anti-Renters, and a thousand other agrarian sects that have arisen in these countries, and threaten to subvert the whole social fabric. The leaders of these sects, at least in France, comprise within their ranks the greater number of the most cultivated and profound minds in the nation, who have made government their study. Add to the evidence of these social philosophers, who, watching closely the working of the system, have proclaimed to the world its total failure, the condition of the working classes, and we have conclusive proof that liberty and equality have not conduced to enhance the comfort or the happiness of the people. Crime and pauperism have increased. Riots, trade unions, strikes for higher wages, discontent breaking out into revolution, are things of daily occurrence, and show that the poor see and feel quite as clearly as the philosophers, that their condition is far worse under the new than under the old order of things. . . .

Liberty and equality have not [enhanced] the comfort or the happiness of the people.

So much for experiment. We will now endeavor to treat the subject theoretically, and to show that the system is on its face self-destructive and impracticable. When we look to the vegetable, animal and human kingdoms, we discover in them all a constant conflict, war, or race of competition, the result of which is, that the weaker or less healthy genera, species and individuals are continually displaced and exterminated by the stronger and more hardy. It is a means by which some contend Nature is perfecting her own work. We, however, witness the war, but do not see the improvement. Although from the earliest date of recorded history, one race of plants has been eating out and taking the place of another, the stronger or more cunning animals have been destroying the feebler, and man exterminating and supplanting his fellow, still the plants, the animals and the men of to-day seem not at all superior, even in those qualities of strength and hardihood to which they owe their continued existence, to those of thousands of years ago. To this propensity of the strong to oppress and destroy the weak, government owes its existence. So strong is this propensity, and so destructive to human existence, that man has never yet been found so savage as to be without government. Forgetful of this important fact, which is the origin of all governments, the political economists and the advocates of liberty and equality propose to enhance the well being of man by trammeling his conduct as little as possible, and encouraging what they call FREE COMPETITION. Now, free competition is but another name for liberty and equality, and we must acquire precise and accurate notions about it in order to ascertain how free institutions will work. It is, then, that war or conflict to which Nature impels her creatures, and which government was intended to restrict. It is true, it is that war somewhat modified and restricted, for the warmest friends of freedom would have some government. The question is, whether the proposed restrictions are sufficient to neutralize the self-destructive tendencies which nature impresses on society. We proceed to show that the war of the wits, of mind with mind, which free competition or liberty and equality beget and encourage, is quite as oppressive, cruel and exterminating, as the war of the sword, of theft, robbery, and murder, which it forbids. It is only substituting strength of mind for strength of body. Men are told it is their duty to compete, to endeavor to get ahead of and supplant their fellow men, by the exercise of all the intellectual and moral strength with which nature and education have endowed them. "Might makes right," is the order of creation, and this law of nature, so far as mental might is concerned, is restored by liberty to man. The struggle to better one's condition, to pull others down or supplant them, is the great organic law of free society. All men being equal, all aspire to the highest honors and the largest possessions. Good men and bad men teach their children one and the same lesson—"Go ahead, push your way in the world." In such society, virtue, if virtue there be, loses all her loveliness because of her selfish aims. None but the selfish virtues are encouraged, because none other aid a man in the race of free competition. Good men and bad men have the same end in view, are in pursuit of the same object—self-promotion, self-elevation. The good man is prudent, cautious, and cunning of fence; he knows well the arts (the virtues, if you please,) which will advance his fortunes and enable him to depress and supplant others; he bides his time, takes advantage of the follies, the improvidence, and vices of others, and makes his fortune out of the misfortunes of his fellow men. The bad man is rash, hasty, and unskillful. He is equally selfish, but not half so cunning. Selfishness is almost the only motive of human conduct with good and bad in free society, where every man is taught that he may change and better his condition. A vulgar adage, "Every man for himself, and devil take the hindmost," is the moral which liberty and free competition inculcate. Now, there are no more honors and wealth in proportion to numbers, in this generation, than in the one which preceded it; population fully keeps pace with the means of subsistence; hence, those who better their condition or rise to higher places in society, do so generally by pulling down others or pushing them from their places. Where men of strong minds, of strong wills, and of great self-control, come into free competition with the weak and improvident, the latter soon become the inmates of jails and penitentiaries.

The Effects of Liberty and Equality

The statistics of France, England and America show that pauperism and crime advance *pari passu* [side by side] with liberty and equality. How can it be otherwise, when all society is combined to oppress the poor and weak minded? The rich man, however good he may be, employs the laborer who will work for the least wages. If he be a good man, his punctuality enables him to cheapen the wages of the poor man. The poor war with one another in the race of competition, in order to get employment, by underbidding; for laborers are more abundant than employers. Population increases faster than capital. . . .

Slaves never die of hunger, scarcely ever feel want.

We do not set children and women free because they are not capable of taking care of themselves, not equal to the constant struggle of society. To set them free would be to give the lamb to the wolf to take care of. Society would quickly devour them. If the children of ten years of age

were remitted to all the rights of person and property
which men enjoy, all can perceive how soon ruin and
penury would overtake them. But half of mankind are but
grown-up children, and liberty is as fatal to them as it
would be to children. . . .

---

*There is no rivalry, no competition to get
employment among slaves, as among free
laborers.*

One step more, and that the most difficult in this
process of reasoning and illustration, and we have done with
this part of our subject. Liberty and equality throw the
whole weight of society on its weakest members; they combine all men in oppressing precisely that part of mankind
who most need sympathy, aid and protection. The very astute and avaricious man, when left free to exercise his facul-
ties, is injured by no one in the field of competition, but
levies a tax on all with whom he deals. The sensible and prudent, but less astute man, is seldom worsted in competing
with his fellow men, and generally benefited. The very simple and improvident man is the prey of every body. The
simple man represents a class, the common day laborers.
The employer cheapens their wages, and the retail dealer
takes advantage of their ignorance, their inability to visit
other markets, and their want of credit, to charge them
enormous profits. They bear the whole weight of society on
their shoulders; they are the producers and artificers of all
the necessaries, the comforts, the luxuries, the pomp and
splendor of the world; they create it all, and enjoy none of
it; they are the muzzled ox that treadeth out the straw; they
are at constant war with those above them, asking higher
wages but getting lower; for they are also at war with each
other, underbidding to get employment. This process of
underbidding never ceases so long as employers want profits or laborers want employment. It ends when wages are reduced too low to afford subsistence, in filling poor-houses,
and jails, and graves. It has reached that point already in
France, England and Ireland. A half million died of hunger
in one year in Ireland—they died because in the eye of the
law they were the equals, and liberty had made them the enemies, of their landlords and employers. Had they been vas-

sals or serfs, they would have been beloved, cherished and taken care of by those same landlords and employers. Slaves never die of hunger, scarcely ever feel want.

The bestowing upon men equality of rights, is but giving license to the strong to oppress the weak. It begets the grossest inequalities of condition. Menials and day laborers are and must be as numerous as in a land of slavery. And these menials and laborers are only taken care of while young, strong and healthy. If the laborer gets sick, his wages cease just as his demands are greatest. If two of the poor get married, who being young and healthy, are getting good wages, in a few years they may have four children. Their wants have increased, but the mother has enough to do to nurse the four children, and the wages of the husband must support six. There is no equality, except in theory, in such society, and there is no liberty. The men of property, those who own lands and money, are masters of the poor; masters, with none of the feelings, interests or sympathies of masters; they employ them when they please, and for what they please, and may leave them to die in the highway, for it is the only home to which the poor in free countries are entitled. . . .

Slavery and High Civilization

To it (slavery) Greece and Rome, Egypt and Judea, and all the other distinguished States of antiquity, were indebted for their great prosperity and high civilization. . . .

But this high civilization and domestic slavery did not merely co-exist, they were cause and effect. Every scholar whose mind is at all imbued with ancient history and literature, sees that Greece and Rome were indebted to this institution [slavery] alone for the taste, the leisure and the means to cultivate their heads and their hearts; had they been tied down to Yankee notions of thrift, they might have produced a Franklin, with his "penny saved is a penny gained"; they might have had utilitarian philosophers and invented the spinning jenny, but they never would have produced a poet, an orator, a sculptor or an architect; they would never have uttered a lofty sentiment, achieved a glorious feat in war, or created a single work of art. . . .

Domestic slavery in the Southern States has produced the same results in elevating the character of the master that it did in Greece and Rome. He is lofty and independent in his sentiments, generous, affectionate, brave and eloquent;

he is superior to the Northerner in every thing but the arts of thrift. . . .

The Condition of the Slave

But the chief and far most important enquiry [sic] is, how does slavery affect the condition of the slave? One of the wildest sects of Communists in France proposes not only to hold all property in common, but to divide the profits, not according to each man's input and labor, but according to each man's wants. Now this is precisely the system of domestic slavery with us. We provide for each slave, in old age and in infancy, in sickness and in health, not according to his labor, but according to his wants. The master's wants are more costly and refined, and he therefore gets a larger share of the profits. A Southern farm is the beau ideal of Communism; it is a joint concern, in which the slave consumes more than the master, of the coarse products, and is far happier, because although the concern may fail, he is always sure of a support; he is only transferred to another master to participate in the profits of another concern; he marries when he pleases, because he knows he will have to work no more with a family than without one, and whether he live or die, that family will be taken care of; he exhibits all the pride of ownership, despises a partner in a smaller concern, "a poor man's negro," boasts of "our crops, horses, fields and cattle"; and is as happy as a human being can be. And why should he not?—he enjoys as much of the fruits of the farm as he is capable of doing, and the wealthiest can do no more. Great wealth brings many additional cares, but few additional enjoyments. Our stomachs do not increase in capacity with our fortunes. We want no more clothing to keep us warm. We may create new wants, but we cannot create new pleasures. The intellectual enjoyments which wealth affords are probably balanced by the new cares it brings along with it.

There is no rivalry, no competition to get employment among slaves, as among free laborers. Nor is there a war between master and slave. The master's interest prevents his reducing the slave's allowance or wages in infancy or sickness, for he might lose the slave by so doing. His feeling for his slave never permits him to stint him in old age. The slaves are all well fed, well clad, have plenty of fuel, and are happy. They have no dread of the future—no fear of want. A state of dependence is the only condition in which reciprocal affection can exist among human beings—the only situation in which the war of competition ceases, and peace, amity and good will arise. A state of independence always begets more or less of jealous rivalry and hostility. A man loves his children because they are weak, helpless and dependent. He loves his wife for similar reasons. When his children grow up and assert their independence, he is apt to transfer his affection to his grandchildren. He ceases to love his wife when she becomes masculine or rebellious; but slaves are always dependent, never the rivals of their master. Hence, though men are often found at variance with wife or children, we never saw one who did not like his slaves, and rarely a slave who was not devoted to his master. . . .

We have no mobs, no trades unions, no strikes for higher wages, no armed resistance to the law, [very] little jealousy of the rich by the poor.

Every social structure must have its substratum [lower class]. In free society this substratum, the weak, poor and ignorant, is borne down upon and oppressed with continually increasing weight by all above. We have solved the problem of relieving this substratum from the pressure from above. The slaves are the substratum, and the master's feelings and interests alike prevent him from bearing down upon and oppressing them. With us the pressure on society is like that of air or water, so equally diffused as not any where to be felt. With them it is the pressure of the enormous screw, never yielding, continually increasing. Free laborers are little better than trespassers on this earth given by God to all mankind. The birds of the air have nests, and the foxes have holes, but they have not where to lay their heads. They are driven to cities to dwell in damp and crowded cellars, and thousands are even forced to lie in the open air. This accounts for the rapid growth of Northern cities. . . .

In France, England, Scotland and Ireland, the genius [inclination] of famine hovers o'er the land. Emigrants, like a flock of hungry pigeons or Egyptian locusts, are alighting on the North. Every green thing will soon be consumed. The hollow, bloated prosperity which she now enjoys is destined soon to pass away. Her wealth does not increase with her numbers; she is dependent for the very necessaries of life on the slaveholding States. If those States cut off commercial intercourse with her, as they certainly will do if she does not speedily cease interference with slavery, she will be without food or clothing for her overgrown population. She is already threatened with a social revolution. . . .

North versus South

At the slaveholding South all is peace, quiet, plenty and contentment. We have no mobs, no trades unions, no strikes for higher wages, no armed resistance to the law, but little jealousy of the rich by the poor. We have but few in our jails, and fewer in our poor houses. We produce enough of the comforts and necessaries of life for a population three or four times as numerous as ours. We are wholly exempt from the torrent of pauperism, crime, agrarianism, and infidelity which Europe is pouring from her jails and alms houses on the already crowded North. Population increases slowly, wealth rapidly. . . . Wealth is more equally distributed than at the North, where a few millionaires own most of the property of the country. (These millionaires are men of cold hearts and weak minds; they know how to make money, but not how to use it, either for the benefit of themselves or of others.) High intellectual and moral attainments, refinement of head and heart, give standing to a man in the South, however poor he may be. Money is, with few exceptions, the only thing that ennobles at the North. We have poor among us, but none who are over-worked and under-fed. We do not crowd cities because lands are abundant and their owners kind, merciful and hospitable. The poor are as hospitable as the rich, the negro as the white man. Nobody dreams of turning a friend, a relative, or a stranger from his door. The very negro who deems it no crime to steal, would scorn to sell his hospitality. We have no loafers, because the poor relative or friend who borrows our horse, or spends a week under our roof, is a welcome guest. The loose economy, the wasteful mode of living at the South, is a blessing when rightly considered; it keeps want, scarcity and famine at a distance, because it leaves room for retrenchment. The nice, accurate economy of France, England and New England, keeps society always on the verge of famine, because it leaves no room to retrench, that is to live on a part only of what they now consume. Our society exhibits no appearance of precocity [aging before its time], no symptoms of decay. A long course of continuing improvement is in prospect before us, with no limits which human foresight can descry. Actual liberty and equality with our white population has been approached much nearer than in the free States. Few of our whites ever work as day laborers, none as cooks, scullions, ostlers, body servants, or in other menial capacities. One free citizen does not lord it over another; hence that feeling of independence and equality that distinguishes us; hence that pride of character, that self-respect, that gives us ascendancy when we come in contact with Northerners. It is a distinction to be a Southerner, as it was once to be a Roman citizen. . . .

The Defects of the New System

In conclusion, we will repeat the propositions, in somewhat different phraseology, with which we set out. First—That Liberty and Equality, with their concomitant Free Competition, beget a war in society that is as destructive to its weaker members as the custom of exposing the deformed and crippled children. Secondly—That slavery protects the weaker members of society just as do the relations of parent, guardian and husband, and is as necessary, as natural, and almost as universal as those relations. Is our demonstration imperfect? Does universal experience sustain our theory? Should the conclusions to which we have arrived appear strange and startling, let them therefore not be rejected without examination. The world has had but little opportunity to contrast the working of Liberty and Equality with the old order of things, which always partook more or less of the character of domestic slavery. The strong prepossession in the public mind in favor of the new system, makes it reluctant to attribute the evil phenomena which it exhibits, to defects inherent in the system itself. That these defects should not have been foreseen and pointed out by any process of *a priori* [logical] reasoning—is but another proof of the fallibility of human sagacity [wisdom] and foresight when attempting to foretell the operation of new institutions. It is as much as human reason can do, when examining the complex frame of society, to trace effects back to their causes—much more than it can do, to foresee what effects new causes will produce. We invite investigation.

4

The Territories Should Be Allowed to Decide Their Own Policy on Slavery

Stephen Douglas

In 1858, Abraham Lincoln challenged Stephen Douglas, his rival in the Illinois Senate race, to a series of debates. The primary focus of the first debate was the territories: Should slaveholding be allowed in them or outlawed? Douglas, as the author of the Kansas-Nebraska Act, promoted the idea of "popular sovereignty" for the territories. He believed that those living in the territorial regions were capable of deciding for themselves whether slavery would be allowed in their region. Whether the inhabitants of the Kansas-Nebraska territory eventually voted for or against allowing slavery, Douglas did not consider the decision to be a threat to the stability and existence of the Union. The following are excerpts of Douglas's remarks from the first Lincoln/Douglas debate, held on August 21, 1858, in Ottawa, Illinois.

---

*L*adies and gentlemen: I appear before you to-day for the purpose of discussing the leading political topics which now agitate the public mind. By an arrangement between Mr. Lincoln and myself, we are present here to-day for the purpose of having a joint discussion as the representatives of the two great political parties of the State and Union, upon the principles in issue between these parties and this vast concourse of people, shows the deep feeling which pervades the public mind in regard to the questions dividing us. . . .

Stephen Douglas, debate with Abraham Lincoln, Ottawa, Illinois, August 21, 1858.

The Issue of the Territories

During the session of Congress of 1853–'54, I introduced into the Senate of the United States a bill to organize the Territories of Kansas and Nebraska on that principle which had been adopted in the compromise measures of 1850, approved by the Whig party and the Democratic party in Illinois in 1851, and endorsed by the Whig party and the Democratic party in national convention in 1852. In order that there might be no misunderstanding in relation to the principle involved in the Kansas and Nebraska bill, I put forth the true intent and meaning of the act in these words: "It is the true intent and meaning of this act not to legislate slavery into any State or Territory, or to exclude it therefrom, but to leave the people thereof perfectly free to form and regulate their domestic institutions in their own way, subject only to the federal constitution." Thus, you see, that up to 1854, when the Kansas and Nebraska bill was brought into Congress for the purpose of carrying out the principles which both parties had up to that time endorsed and approved, there had been no division in this country in regard to that principle except the opposition of the abolitionists. In the House of Representatives of the Illinois Legislature, upon a resolution asserting that principle, every Whig and every Democrat in the House voted in the affirmative, and only four men voted against it, and those four were old line Abolitionists. . . .

Douglas Questions Lincoln

I desire him [Abraham Lincoln] to answer whether he stands pledged to-day, as he did in 1854, against the admission of any more slave States into the Union, even if the people want them. I want to know whether he stands pledged against the admission of a new State into the Union with such a constitution as the people of that State may see fit to make. I want to know whether he stands to-day pledged to the abolition of slavery in the District of Columbia. I desire him to answer whether he stands pledged to the prohibition of the slave trade between the different States. I desire to know whether he stands pledged to prohibit slavery in all the territories of the United States, North as well as South of the Missouri Compromise line. I desire him to answer whether he is opposed to the acquisition of any more territory unless slavery is first prohibited therein. I want his answer to these questions. Your affirmative cheers in favor of this Abolition platform is not satisfactory. I ask Abraham Lincoln to answer these questions, in order that when I trot him down to lower Egypt I may put the same questions to him. My principles are the same everywhere. I can proclaim them alike in the North, the South, the East, and the West. My principles will apply wherever the Constitution prevails and the American flag waves. I desire to know whether Mr. Lincoln's principles will bear transplanting from Ottawa to Jonesboro? I put these questions to him to-day distinctly, and ask an answer. I have a right to an answer, for I quote from the platform of the Republican party, made by himself and others at the time that party was formed, and the bargain made by Lincoln to dissolve and kill the old Whig party, and transfer its members, bound hand and foot, to the Abolition [Republican] party, under the direction of [Joshua R.] Giddings and Fred Douglass. In the remarks I have made on this platform, and the position of Mr. Lincoln upon it, I mean nothing personally disrespectful or unkind to that gentleman. I have known him for nearly twenty-five years. There were many points of sympathy between us when we first got acquainted. . . .

Lincoln's Abolition Doctrines

Having formed this new [Republican] party for the benefit of deserters from Whiggery, and deserters from Democracy, and having laid down the Abolition platform which I have read, Lincoln now takes his stand and proclaims his Abolition doctrines. Let me read a part of them. In his speech at Springfield to the convention which nominated him for the Senate, he said:

> In my opinion it will not cease until a crisis shall have been reached and passed. "A house divided against itself cannot stand." I believe this Government *cannot endure permanently half Slave and half Free.* I do not expect the Union to be dissolved—I do not expect the house to fall—*but I do expect it will cease to be divided.* It will become all one thing, or all the other. Either the opponents of Slavery *will arrest the further spread of it,* and place it where the public mind shall rest in the belief *that it is in the course of ultimate extinction;* or its advocates *will push it forward till it shall become alike lawful in all the States*—old as well as new, North as well as South.

I am delighted to hear you Black Republicans say "good." I have no doubt that doctrine expresses your sentiments and I will prove to you now, if you will listen to me, that it is revolutionary and destructive of the existence of this Government. Mr. Lincoln, in the extract from which I have read, says that this Government cannot endure permanently in the same condition in which it was made by its framers—divided into free and slave States. He says that it has existed for about seventy years thus divided, and yet he tells you that it cannot endure permanently on the same principles and in the same relative condition in which our fathers made it. Why can it not exist divided into free and slave States? Washington, Jefferson, Franklin, Madison, Hamilton, Jay, and the great men of that day, made this Government divided into free States and slave States, and left each State perfectly free to do as it pleased on the subject of slavery. Why can it not exist on the same principles on which our fathers made it? They knew when they framed the Constitution that in a country as wide and broad as this, with such a variety of climate, production and interest, the people necessarily required different laws and institutions in different localities. They knew that the laws and regulations which would suit the granite hills of New Hampshire would be unsuited to the rice plantations of South Carolina, and they, therefore, provided that each State should retain its own Legislature, and its own sovereignty with the full and complete power to do as it pleased within its own limits, in all that was local and not national. One of the reserved rights of the States, was the right to regulate the relations between Master and Servant, on the slavery question. At the time the Constitution was formed, there were thirteen States in the Union, twelve of which were slaveholding States and one a free State. Suppose this doctrine of uniformity preached by Mr. Lincoln, that the States should all be free or all be slave had prevailed and what would have been the result? Of course, the twelve slaveholding States would have overruled the one free State, and slavery would have been fastened by a Constitutional provision on every inch of the American Republic, instead of being left as our fathers wisely left it, to each State to decide for itself. Here I assert that uniformity in the local laws and institutions of the different States is neither possible or desirable. If uniformity had been adopted when the government was established, it must inevitably have been the uniformity of slavery everywhere, or else the uniformity of negro citizenship and negro equality everywhere. . . .

The Negro Question

If you desire negro citizenship, if you desire to allow them to come into the State and settle with the white man, if you desire them to vote on an equality with yourselves, and to make them eligible to office, to serve on juries, and to adjudge your rights, then support Mr. Lincoln and the Black Republican party, who are in favor of the citizenship of the negro. For one, I am opposed to negro citizenship in any and every form. I believe this government was made on the white basis. I believe it was made by white men, for the benefit of white men and their posterity for ever, and I am in favor of confining citizenship to white men, men of European birth and descent, instead of conferring it upon negroes, Indians and other inferior races.

I desire to know whether he stands pledged to prohibit slavery in all the territories of the United States.

Mr. Lincoln, following the example and lead of all the little Abolition orators, who go around and lecture in the basements of schools and churches, reads from the Declaration of Independence, that all men were created equal, and then asks how can you deprive a negro of that equality which God and the Declaration of Independence awards to him. He and they maintain that negro equality is guarantied by the laws of God, and that it is asserted in the Declaration of Independence. If they think so, of course they have a right to say so, and so vote. I do not question Mr. Lincoln's conscientious belief that the negro was made his equal, and hence is his brother, but for my own part, I do not regard the negro as my equal, and positively deny that he is my brother or any kin to me whatever. . . . He belongs to an inferior race, and must always occupy an inferior position. I do not hold that because the negro is our inferior that therefore he ought to be a slave. By no means can such a conclusion be drawn from what I have said. On the contrary, I hold that humanity and christianity both require that the negro shall have and enjoy every right, every privilege, and every immunity consistent with the safety of the society in which he lives. On that point, I presume, there can be no diversity of opinion. You and I are bound to extend to our inferior and dependent being every right, every privilege, every facility and immunity consistent with the public good. The question then arises what rights and privileges are consistent with the public good. This is a question which each State and each Territory must decide for itself—Illinois has decided it for herself. We have provided that the negro shall not be a slave, and we have also provided that he shall not be a citizen, but protect him in his civil rights, in his life, his person and his property, only depriving him of all political rights whatsoever, and refusing to put him on an equality with the white man. That policy of Illinois is satisfactory to the Democratic party and to me, and if it were to the Republicans, there would then be no question upon the subject; but the Republicans say that he ought to be made a citizen, and when he becomes a citizen he becomes your equal, with all your rights and privileges. They assert the Dred Scott decision to be monstrous because it denies that the negro is or can be a citizen under the Constitution. Now, I hold that Illinois had a right to abolish and prohibit slavery as she did, and I hold that Kentucky has the same right to continue and protect slavery that Illinois had to abolish it. I hold that New York had as much right to abolish slavery as Virginia has to continue it, and that each and every State of this Union is a sovereign power, with the right to do as it pleases upon this question of slavery, and upon all its domestic institutions. Slavery is not the only question which comes up in this controversy. There is a far more important one to you, and that is, what shall be done with the free negro? We have settled the slavery question as far as we are concerned; we have prohibited it in Illinois forever, and in doing so, I think we have done wisely, and there is no man in the State who would be more strenuous in his opposition to the introduction of slavery than I would; but when we settled it for ourselves, we exhausted all our power over that subject. We have done our whole duty, and can do no more. We must leave each and every other State to decide for itself the same question. . . .

Now, my friends, if we will only act conscientiously and rigidly upon this great principle of popular sovereignty which guarantees to each State and Territory the right to do as it pleases on all things local and domestic instead of Congress interfering, we will continue at peace one with another. Why should Illinois be at war with Missouri, or Kentucky with Ohio, or Virginia with New York, merely because their institutions differ? Our fathers intended that our institutions should differ. They knew that the North and the South having different climates, productions and interests, required different institutions. This doctrine of Mr. Lincoln's of uniformity among the institutions of the different States is a new doctrine, never dreamed of by Washington, Madison, or the framers of this Government. Mr. Lincoln and the Republican party set themselves up as wiser than these men who made this government, which has flourished for seventy years under the principle of popular sovereignty, recognizing the right of each State to do as it pleased. Under that principle, we have grown from a nation of three or four millions to a nation of about thirty millions of people; we have crossed the Allegheny mountains and filled up the whole North West, turning the prairie into a garden, and building up churches and schools, thus spreading civilization and christianity where before there was nothing but savage-barbarism. Under that principle we have become from a feeble nation, the most powerful on the face of the earth, and if we only adhere to that principle, we can go forward increasing in territory, in power, in strength and in glory until the Republic of America shall be the North Star that shall guide the friends of freedom throughout the civilized world. And why can we not adhere to the great principle of self-government, upon which our institutions were originally based. I believe that this new doctrine preached by Mr. Lincoln and his party will dissolve the Union if it succeeds. They are trying to array all the Northern States in one body against the South, to excite a sectional war between the free States and the slave States, in order that the one or the other may be driven to the wall.

5

Slavery Should Not Spread into the Territories

Abraham Lincoln

In 1858, during the first of a series of political debates between Abraham Lincoln and Stephen Douglas, Lincoln stated that he was opposed to the institution of slavery and believed that the new territories should be free of slaveholding. He was just as adamant in his belief that the issue of slavery was a threat to the peace—and the very existence—of the Union. The debates did not end as Lincoln had planned: He lost the Senate race to Douglas. However, these debates did have the greater effect of pushing Lincoln into national political prominence—in 1860 he became the Republican nominee for president of the United States.

N ow gentlemen, I hate to waste my time on such things, but in regard to that general abolition tilt that Judge Douglas makes, when he says that I was engaged at that time in selling out and abolitionizing the old Whig party— I hope you will permit me to read a part of a printed speech that I made then at Peoria, which will show altogether a different view of the position I took in that contest of 1854. . . .

> This is the *repeal* of the Missouri Compromise. The foregoing history may not be precisely accurate in every particular; but I am sure it is sufficiently so, for all the uses I shall attempt to make of it, and in it, we have before us, the chief materials enabling us to cor-

Abraham Lincoln, debate with Stephen Douglas, Ottawa, Illinois, August 21, 1858.

rectly judge whether the repeal of the Missouri Compromise is right or wrong.

I think, and shall try to show, that it is wrong; wrong in its direct effect, letting slavery into Kansas and Nebraska—and wrong in its prospective principle, allowing it to spread to every other part of the wide world, where men can be found inclined to take it.

This *declared* indifference, but as I must think, covert *real* zeal for the spread of slavery, I can not but hate. I hate it because of the monstrous injustice of slavery itself. I hate it because it deprives our republican example of its just influence in the world—enables the enemies of free institutions, with plausibility, to taunt us as hypocrites—causes the real friends of freedom to doubt our sincerity, and especially because it forces so many really good men amongst ourselves into an open war with the very fundamental principles of civil liberty—criticising the Declaration of Independence, and insisting that there is no right principle of action but *self-interest.*

Before proceeding, let me say I think I have no prejudice against the Southern people. They are just what we would be in their situation. If slavery did not now exist amongst them, they would not introduce it. If it did now exist amongst us, we should not instantly give it up. This I believe of the masses north and south. Doubtless there are individuals, on both sides, who would not hold slaves under any circumstances; and others who would gladly introduce slavery anew, if it were out of existence. We know that some southern men do free their slaves, go north, and become tip-top abolitionists; while some northern ones go south, and become most cruel slave-masters.

When southern people tell us they are no more responsible for the origin of slavery, than we; I acknowledge the fact. When it is said that the institution exists, and that it is very difficult to get rid of it, in any satisfactory way, I can understand and appreciate the saying. I surely will not blame them for not doing what I should not know how to do myself. If all earthly power were given me, I should not know what to do, as to the existing institution. My first impulse would be to free all the slaves, and send them to Liberia,—to their own native land. But a moment's reflection would convince me, that whatever of high hope, (as I think there is) there may be in this, in the long run, its sudden execution is impossible. If they were all landed there in a day, they would all perish in the next ten days; and there are not surplus shipping and surplus money enough in the world to carry them there in many times ten days. What then? Free them all, and keep them among us as underlings? Is it quite certain that this betters their condition? I think I would not hold one in slavery, at any rate; yet the point is not clear enough to me to denounce people upon. What next? Free them, and make them politically and socially, our equals? My own feelings will not admit of this; and if mine would, we well know that those of the great mass of white people will not. Whether this feeling accords with justice and sound judgment, is not the sole question, if indeed, it is any part of it. A universal feeling, whether well or ill-founded, can not be safely disregarded. We can not, then, make them equals. It does seem to me that systems of gradual emancipation might be adopted; but for their tardiness in this, I will not undertake to judge our brethren of the south.

When they remind us of their constitutional rights, I acknowledge them, not grudgingly, but fully, and fairly; and I would give them any legislation for the reclaiming of their fugitives, which should not, in its stringency, be more likely to carry a free man into slavery, than our ordinary criminal laws are to hang an innocent one.

But all this; to my judgment, furnishes no more excuse for permitting slavery to go into our own free territory, than it would for reviving the African slave trade by law. The law which forbids the bringing of slaves *from* Africa; and that which has so long forbid the taking them *to* Nebraska, can hardly be distinguished on any moral principle; and the repeal of the former could find quite as plausible excuses as that of the latter.

I have reason to know that Judge Douglas *knows* that I said this. I think he has the answer here to one of the questions he put to me. I do not mean to allow him to catechise me unless he pays back for it in kind. I will not answer questions one after another unless he reciprocates, but as he made this inquiry and I have answered it before, he has got it without my getting anything in return.

The Negro and Natural Rights

Now gentlemen, I don't want to read at any greater length, but this is the true complexion of all I have ever said in regard to the institution of slavery and the black race. This is the whole of it, and anything that argues me into his idea of perfect social and political equality with the negro, is but a specious and fantastic arrangement of words, by which a man can prove a horse chestnut to be a chestnut horse. I will say here, while upon this subject, that I have no purpose directly or indirectly to interfere with the institution of slavery in the States where it exists. I believe I have no lawful right to do so, and I have no inclination to do so. I have no purpose to introduce political and social equality between the white and the black races. There is a physical difference between the two, which in my judgment will probably forever forbid their living together upon the footing of perfect equality, and inasmuch as it becomes a necessity that there must be a difference, I, as well as Judge Douglas, am in favor of the race to which I belong, having the superior position. I have never said anything to the contrary, but I hold that notwithstanding all this, there is no reason in the world why the negro is not entitled to all the natural rights enumerated in the Declaration of Independence, the right to life, liberty and the pursuit of happiness. I hold that he is as much entitled to these as the white man. I agree with Judge Douglas he is not my equal in many respects—certainly not in color, perhaps not in moral or intellectual endowment. But in the right to eat the bread, without leave of anybody else, which his own hand earns, *he is my equal and the equal of Judge Douglas, and the equal of every living man.* . . .

"A House Divided" and the Territories

As I have not used up so much of my time as I had supposed, I will dwell a little longer upon one or two of these minor topics upon which the Judge has spoken. He has read from my speech in Springfield, in which I say that "a house divided against itself cannot stand." Does the Judge say it *can* stand? I don't know whether he does or not. The Judge does not seem to be attending to me just now, but I would like to know if it is his opinion that a house divided against itself *can stand*. If he does, then there is a question of veracity, not between him and me, but between the Judge and an authority of a somewhat higher character.

There is no reason in the world why the negro is not entitled to all the natural rights enumerated in the Declaration of Independence.

Now, my friends, I ask your attention to this matter for the purpose of saying something seriously. I know that the Judge may readily enough agree with me that the maxim which was put forth by the Saviour is true, but he may allege that I misapply it; and the Judge has a right to urge that, in my application, I do misapply it, and then I have a right to show that I do *not* misapply it. When he undertakes to say that because I think this nation, so far as the question of Slavery is concerned, will all become one thing or all the other, I am in favor of bringing about a dead uniformity in the various States, in all their institutions, he argues erroneously. The great variety of the local institutions in the States, springing from differences in the soil, differences in the face of the country, and in the climate, are bonds of Union. They do not make "a house divided against itself," but they make a house united. If they produce in one section of the country what is called for by the wants of another section, and this other section can supply the wants of the first, they are not matters of discord but bonds of union, true bonds of union. But can this question of slavery be considered as among *these* varieties in the institutions of the country? I leave it to you to say whether, in the history of our government, this institution of slavery has not always failed to be a bond of union, and, on the contrary, been an apple of discord and an element of division in the house. I ask you to consider whether, so long as the moral constitution of men's minds shall continue to be the same, after this generation and assemblage shall sink into the grave, and another race shall arise, with the same moral and intellectual development we have—whether, if that institution is standing in the same irritating position in which it now is, it will not continue an element of division? If so, then I have a right to say that in regard to this question, the Union is a house divided against itself, and when the Judge reminds me that I have often said to him that the institution of slavery has existed for eighty years in some States, and yet it does not exist in some others, I agree to the fact, and I account for it by looking at the position in which our fathers originally placed it—restricting it from the new Territories where it had not gone, and legislating to cut off its source by the abrogation of the slave trade, thus putting the seal of legislation *against its spread*. The public mind *did* rest in the belief that it was in the course of ultimate extinction. But lately, I think—and in this I charge nothing on the Judge's motives—lately, I think, that he, and those acting with him, have placed that institution on a new basis, which looks to the *perpetuity and nationalization of slavery*. And while it is placed upon this new basis, I say, and I have said, that I believe we shall not have peace upon the question until the opponents of slavery arrest the further spread of it, and place it where the public mind shall rest in the belief that it is in the course of ultimate extinction; or, on the other hand, that its advocates will push it forward until it shall become alike lawful in all the States, old as well as new, North as well as South. Now, I believe if we could arrest the spread, and place it where Washington, and Jefferson, and Madison placed it, it *would be* in the course of ultimate extinction, and the public mind *would*, as for eighty years past, believe that it was in the course of ultimate extinction. The crisis would be past and the institution might be let alone for a hundred years, if it should live so long, in the States where it exists, yet it would be going out of existence in the way best for both the black and the white races. . . .

Popular Sovereignty

Well, then, let us talk about Popular Sovereignty! What is Popular Sovereignty? Is it the right of the people to have Slavery or not have it, as they see fit, in the territories? I will state—and I have an able man to watch me—my understanding is that Popular Sovereignty, as now applied to the question of Slavery, does allow the people of a Territory to have Slavery if they want to, but does not allow them *not* to have it if they *do not* want it. I do not mean that if this vast concourse of people were in a Territory of the United States, any one of them would be obliged to have a slave if he did not want one; but I do say that, as I understand the Dred Scott decision, if any one man wants slaves, all the rest have no way of keeping that one man from holding them.

I believe we shall not have peace upon the question until the opponents of slavery arrest the further spread of it.

When I made my speech at Springfield, of which the Judge complains, and from which he quotes, I really was not thinking of the things which he ascribes to me at all. I had no thought in the world that I was doing anything to bring about a war between the free and slave States. I had no thought in the world that I was doing anything to bring about a political and social equality of the black and white races. It never occurred to me that I was doing anything or favoring anything to reduce to a dead uniformity all the local institutions of the various States. . . . But can it be true, that placing this institution upon the original basis—the basis upon which our fathers placed it—can have any tendency to set the Northern and the Southern States at war with one another, or that it can have any tendency to make the people of Vermont raise sugar cane, because they raise it in Louisiana, or that it can compel the people of Illinois to cut pine logs on the Grand Prairie, where they will not grow, because they cut pine logs in Maine, where they do grow? The Judge says this is a new principle started in regard to this question. Does the Judge claim that he is working on the plan of the founders of government? I think he says in some of his speeches—indeed I have one here now—that he saw evidence of a policy to allow slavery to be south of a certain line, while north of it it should be excluded, and he saw an indisposition on the part of the country to stand upon that policy, and therefore he set about studying the subject upon *original principles*, and upon *original principles* he got up the Nebraska bill! I am fighting it upon these "original principles"—fighting it in the Jeffersonian, Washingtonian, and Madisonian fashion.

Now my friends I wish you to attend for a little while to

one or two other things in that Springfield speech. My main object was to show, so far as my humble ability was capable of showing to the people of this country, what I believed was the truth—that there was a *tendency*, if not a conspiracy among those who have engineered this slavery question for the last four or five years, to make slavery perpetual and universal in this nation. . . .

My Opponent and Popular Sovereignty

I want to ask your attention to a portion of the Nebraska Bill, which Judge Douglas has quoted: "It being the true intent and meaning of this act, not to legislate slavery into any Territory or State, nor to exclude it therefrom, but to leave the people thereof perfectly free to form and regulate their domestic institutions in their own way, subject only to the Constitution of the United States." Thereupon Judge Douglas and others began to argue in favor of "Popular Sovereignty"—the right of the people to have slaves if they wanted them, and to exclude slavery if they did not want them. "But," said, in substance, a Senator from Ohio, (Mr. Chase, I believe,) "we more than suspect that you do not mean to allow the people to exclude slavery if they wish to, and if you do mean it, accept an amendment which I propose expressly authorizing the people to exclude slavery." I believe I have the amendment here before me, which was offered, and under which the people of the Territory, through their proper representatives, might if they saw fit, prohibit the existence of slavery therein. And now I state it as a *fact*, to be taken back if there is any mistake about it, that Judge Douglas and those acting with him, *voted that amendment down.* . . .

When [Judge Douglas] says he "cares not whether slavery is voted down or voted up,"—that it is a sacred right of self government—he is in my judgment penetrating the human soul and eradicating the light of reason and the love of liberty in this American people.

6

The Fugitive Slave Law Can Heal the Nation

Henry Clay

By 1850, the United States was divided over the issue of whether slavery should be allowed in any new states or territories. The introduction and passage of the Compromise of 1850 by the U.S. Congress was a desperate attempt to heal the nation and, according to one of the bill's creators, Kentucky senator Henry Clay, "restore . . . peace to this great country." Among its provisions, the compromise abolished the trading of slaves in Washington, D.C., and made California a part of the Union as a free state. In addition, this bill strengthened the previously enacted Fugitive Slave Law. As described in the following excerpt from a speech given by Clay, that portion of the compromise required all escaped slaves to be returned to their owners aided not only by federal officers but by private citizens as well. It was Clay's intention that an invigorated Fugitive Slave Law would stem the mounting frictions between the states over the issue of slavery.

From the beginning of the session to the present time my thoughts have been anxiously directed to the object of finding some plan, of proposing some mode of accommodation which would once more restore the blessings of concord, harmony, and peace to this great country. . . .

Sir, when I came to consider this subject, there were two or three general purposes which it seemed to me to be most desirable, if possible, to accomplish. The one was, to settle

Henry Clay, speech before the United States Senate, February 5–6, 1850.

all the controverted questions arising out of the subject of slavery. It seemed to me to be doing very little if we settled one question and left other distracting questions unadjusted; it seemed to me to be doing but little if we stopped one leak only in the ship of State, and left other leaks capable of producing danger, if not destruction, to the vessel. I therefore turned my attention to every subject connected with the institution of slavery, and out of which controverted questions had sprung, to see if it were possible or practicable to accommodate and adjust the whole of them. Another principal object which attracted my attention was, to endeavor to form such a scheme of accommodation that neither of the two classes of States into which our country is so unhappily divided should make any sacrifice of any great principle. I believe, sir, the series of resolutions which I have had the honor to present to the Senate accomplishes that object.

My thoughts have been anxiously directed to . . . finding some plan . . . [to] restore the blessings of concord, harmony, and peace to this great country.

Sir, another purpose which I have had in view was this: I was aware of the difference of opinion prevailing between these two classes of States. I was aware that, while one portion of the Union was pushing matters, as it seemed to me, to the greatest extremity, another portion of the Union was pushing them to an opposite, perhaps not less dangerous extremity. It appeared to me, then, that if any arrangement, any satisfactory adjustment could be made of the controverted questions between the two classes of States, that adjustment, that arrangement, could only be successful and effectual by extracting from both parties some concession—not of principle, not of principle at all, but of feeling, of opinion, in relation to matters in controversy between them. . . .

Resolution Proposing the Fugitive Slave Law

The . . . resolution is: "That more effectual provision ought to be made by law, according to the requirement of the Constitution, for the restitution and delivery of persons bound to service or labor in any State, who may escape into any other State or Territory in the Union."

---

*[The U.S. Constitution] imposes an obligation
. . . upon all the people of the United States, . . .
to assist in the surrender and recovery of a
fugitive slave from his master.*

Now, Mr. President, upon that subject I go with him who goes furthest in the interpretation of that clause in the Constitution. In my humble opinion, sir, it is a requirement by the Constitution of the United States which is not limited in its operation to the Congress of the United States, but extends to every State in the Union and to the officers of every State in the Union; and I go one step further: it extends to every man in the Union, and develops upon them all an obligation to assist in the recovery of a fugitive from labor who takes refuge in or escapes into one of the free States. And, sir, I think I can maintain all this by a fair interpretation of the Constitution. It provides:

"That no person held to service or labor in one State under the laws thereof, escaping into another, shall, in consequence of any law or regulation therein, be discharged from service or labor, but shall be delivered up on claim of the party to whom such service or labor may be due."

It will be observed, Mr. President, that this clause in the Constitution is not among the enumerated powers granted to Congress, for, if that had been the case, it might have been urged that Congress alone could legislate to carry it into effect; but it is one of the general powers or one of the general rights secured by this constitutional instrument, and it addresses itself to all who are bound by the Constitution of the United States. Now, sir, the officers of the General Government are bound to take an oath to support the Constitution of the United States. All State officers are required by the Constitution to take an oath to support the Constitution of the United States; and all men who love their country and are obedient to its laws, are bound to assist in the execution of those laws, whether they are fundamental or derivative. I do not say that a private individual is bound to make a tour of his State in order to assist an owner of a slave to recover his property; but I do say, if he is present when the owner of a slave is about to assert his rights and endeavor to obtain possession of his property, every man present, whether he be an officer of the General Government or the State government, or a private individual, is bound to assist, if men are bound at all to assist in the execution of the laws of their country.

Now what is this provision? It is that such fugitive shall be delivered upon claim of the party to whom such service or labor may be due. As has been already remarked in the course of the debate upon the bill upon this subject which is now pending, the language used in regard to fugitives from criminal offenses and fugitives from labor is precisely the same. The fugitive from justice is to be delivered up, and to be removed to the State having jurisdiction; the fugitive from labor is to be delivered up on claim of the party to whom such service is due. Well, has it ever been contended on the part of any State that she is not bound to surrender a fugitive from justice, upon demand from the State from which he fled? I believe not. There have been some exceptions to the performance of this duty, but they have not denied the general right; and if they have refused in any instance to give up the person demanded, it has been upon some technical or legal ground, not at all questioning the general right to have the fugitive surrendered, or the obligation to deliver him up as intended by the Constitution.

I think, then, Mr. President, that with regard to the true interpretation of this provision of the Constitution there can be no doubt. It imposes an obligation upon all the States, free or slaveholding; it imposes an obligation upon all officers of the Government, State or Federal; and, I will add, upon all the people of the United States, under particular circumstances, to assist in the surrender and recovery of a fugitive slave from his master. There has been some confusion and, I think, some misconception, on this subject, in consequence of a recent decision of the Supreme Court of the United States. I think that decision has been entirely misapprehended. There is a vast difference between imposing impediments and affording facilities for the recovery of fugitive slaves. . . .

Mr. President, I do think that that whole class of legislation, beginning in the Northern States and extending to some of the Western States, by which obstructions and impediments have been thrown in the way of the recovery of fugitive slaves, is unconstitutional and has originated in a spirit which I trust will correct itself when those States come calmly to consider the nature and extent of their federal obligations. . . .

I think that the existing laws upon the subject, for the recovery of fugitive slaves, and the restoration and delivering of them up to their owners, being found inadequate and ineffective, it is incumbent on Congress—and I hope hereafter, in a better state of feeling, when more harmony and good will prevail among the members of this confederacy, it will be regarded by the free States themselves as a part of their duty also—to assist in allaying this irritating and disturbing subject to the peace of our Union; but, at all events, whether they do it or not, it is our duty to do it. It is our duty to make the law more effective. . . .

If my plan of peace, and accommodation, and harmony, is not right, present us your plan. Let us see the counter project. Let us see how all the questions that have arisen out of this unhappy subject of slavery can be better settled, more fairly and justly settled to all quarters of the Union.

7

The Fugitive Slave Law Further Divided the Nation

Holman Hamilton

The Fugitive Slave Law had the opposite effect of what its drafters intended. Rather than serving as an instrument of healing for a nation torn apart over the issue of slavery, the act further entrenched opposing viewpoints. In fact, the antislavery movement grew as new converts became disturbed over the manner in which runaway slaves were captured and the lack of due process accorded them as they awaited their return to bondage. Historian Holman Hamilton, in his remarks that follow, argues that few Americans at that time foresaw "the fury of the ensuing tempest." Yet the uproar over this new act, in both the North and the South, became one of the primary forces behind the breakup of the Union.

The Fugitive Slave Law was decidedly the most explosive part of the Compromise [of 1850]. Summary arrangements for determining title to Negroes aroused cries that civil rights were being violated. Doubling the fines formerly assessed against rescuers of runaways was attacked as harsh by vocal critics. The addition of United States commissioners to aid judges in executing the law was assailed with equal ardor. The knowledge that these commissioners received ten dollars for issuing a warrant, but only five for discharging a Negro, was termed a travesty of just procedure. Provocation, too, came from the stipulation that any citizen of the United States was expected to assist officials in apprehending fugitives. As early as September 25, 1850, an Ohio editor prophesied with pleasure that the law "will be a dead letter upon the statute book." In November, another was shocked to hear "men advising their fellow-men to treat a law of Congress as a nullity, and trample its provisions under foot." An editorial in a Maine newspaper, typical of dozens, advocated resistance to the will of Congress and the President. Southern journalists naturally complained. "No sooner has this Fugitive Slave Law gone into effect," wrote a disillusioned Floridian, than "the cry of repeal . . . resounds from one end of the Northern States to the other."

Violent Incidents

Enforced for the first time when only one week old, the law led to a succession of lurid incidents involving desperate runaways, grim agents, fanatical Northerners, and disenchanted Southerners. In February 1851 an escaped slave made his way to a Canadian refuge after a mob bristling with weapons enabled him to flee from a Massachusetts

Under the Fugitive Slave Law, runaway slaves were often treated harshly.

courtroom. Later the same year, the outcome was reversed when a brig from Boston harbor delivered a luckless Georgia Negro to his owner at Savannah. From the eastern seaboard to the Great Lakes region, similar episodes heated the blood. Sometimes bondsmen were dragged back to plantations they hoped never to see again. It was possible— as at Christiana, Pennsylvania, in the dawn of a September morning—for a kindly if credulous Marylander to be killed and mutilated by black men when he tried to regain his property. It was also possible—as at Syracuse in the 1851 "Jerry Rescue" [the rescue of Jerry McHenry]—for New York judges to be defied and sympathizers to chortle and cheer, while fugitives were hidden in private houses and then spirited across the international border.

Feeding Antislavery Fervor

The American who today reads closely the commentary of the *Liberator*, or peruses the *Anti-Slavery Standard* and the *Anti-Slavery Bugle*, can hardly avoid the conclusion that here we have a preeminent model for the pressure politics of the twentieth century. A scholar [Russel B. Nye] has truly written that to the abolitionists the Fugitive Slave Law of 1850 "afforded a common rallying point for all the schisms by which the movement was plagued. Political action men, disunionists, anti-Constitutionalists, non-voters, and non-resistant pacifists found it an issue upon which all could agree." The Jerry Rescue was a *cause célèbre*. As a participant [Samuel J. May] said after it was over, "men that I supposed cared not at all for the enslavement of our colored countrymen, have taken pain to express to me their detestation of the attempt to rob Jerry [McHenry, seized under the Fugitive Slave Law] of his liberty." On this question many a Whig and Democrat who never had sought identification with a [William Lloyd] Garrison or a Gerrit Smith [abolitionists] would react in the same way. Not only did the Fugitive Slave Law intensify extremism, but it broadened the antislavery base as well.

There is no doubt that *Uncle Tom's Cabin*, whose serial publication began in 1851, was inspired by what Harriet Beecher Stowe regarded as an evil law. Ultimately this novel became the most widely read book of the 1850s and one of the century's most influential. The reminder that Mrs. Stowe had little firsthand knowledge of southern life made

no difference whatever to uncritical admirers. Just as the
Fugitive Slave Law (plus maternal loss, religious commit-
ment, and literary ambition) had induced her to venture
into novel-writing, so the same law created an emotional
climate that led her readers to an unquestioning acceptance
of her melodramatic tale. It would be presumptuous to argue that characters like Little Eva, Simon Legree, Mas'r
Haley, and Uncle Tom could not have appeared in print,
had not the Compromise of 1850 and its Fugitive Slave Law
been adopted. But it is indisputable that the book gave a
dramatic form and focus to the passions aroused by the legislation, and the legislation in turn gave an obvious significance to Mrs. Stowe's fable. . . .

---

*The law led to a succession of lurid incidents
involving desperate runaways, grim agents,
fanatical Northerners, and disenchanted
Southerners.*

Propagandists of abolition underscored both pity and
mercy, castigating vile "slave-catchers," making the most of
Negro virtues, and minimizing owners' rights. Occasionally,
they sponsored "rescues" when there was no one to be res-
cued and initiated hunts for "slavers" when the so-called
slavers were rescuers or bystanders. While many were sin-
cere, many found martyrdom appealing. To go to jail, to
stay in jail, and to refuse the payment of fines attracted ide-
alists or sentimentalists whom fervor or notoriety thrust
into prominence. Perhaps the most accurate brief conclusion ever offered on the subject is that [as stated by historian
and author Larry Gara], "after 1850, the pursuit of fugitive
slaves became, like the Fugitive Slave Law itself, more a
symbolic than a practical matter." Both the issue and the law
were of "enormous value in winning sympathy for a once
unpopular movement." Anticipation of that development
probably would have amazed most congressmen in 1850.
Only a tiny portion of their debates was devoted to the
question of fugitive slaves. Indeed, there was no suggestion
then that many of them foresaw the fury of the ensuing
tempest.

Chapter 2

The Secession Crisis

1

A Call to Secession in Response to Lincoln's Election as President

Thomas R.R. Cobb

Considered the "last straw" by many secessionists, Abraham Lincoln's victory in 1860 was a major turning point in the events leading up to the Civil War. Thomas R.R. Cobb, a legal scholar from Georgia, believed Lincoln's election to be unconstitutional and advocated Georgia's "immediate unconditional secession" from the Union. His secession speech, delivered before the Georgia state representatives on November 12, 1860, analyzed Lincoln's victory from a constitutional as well as political point of view. He concluded his remarks by urging his fellow Georgians to act immediately to remove themselves from the Union and preserve their rich heritage as a distinct Southern state.

G entlemen: . . .
In times like these, passion should not rule the hour; calm and dispassionate deliberation should be brought to the consideration of every question. Even the quick beating pulsations of hearts burning with a sense of injuries should be commanded to "be still," while we survey the past, fully appreciate the present, and peer thoughtfully into the future; avoiding the impetuosity of rashness, and the timidity of fears as well, let us invoke all our human wisdom, and light also from on High, to guide us in our decision. But

Thomas R.R. Cobb, speech in Milledgeville, Georgia, November 12, 1860.

once decided, let us act, and act like men, men who are determined to do or die.

It is not necessary for me, in addressing this audience, to rehearse the history of those acts which have so often stirred up our hearts to mutiny, and mantled our faces with shame. You know them as well as I—you have felt them as deeply too. Nor shall I presume you are less patriotic, or need my counseling voice to induce you to remember your homes, or your State. The practical issue before us is the triumph of the sectional Black Republican party of the North, and the duty of Georgia in the present emergency. To this I address myself.

Lincoln's Victory Is Unconstitutional

Is the election of Lincoln a sufficient ground for the dissolution of the Union?

But once decided, let us act, and act like men, men who are determined to do or die.

This may be viewed both as a legal and political question. As a legal question it resolves itself into this. Has he been elected according to the forms and spirit of the Constitution? *Formally*, he has been so elected, when he is so declared by the Congress of the United States. And literally he has been so elected, if the States casting their votes for him are entitled to be counted in the Electoral College; nine of these States, however, casting a combined vote of eighty-five electors, have, by their local legislation, nullified a constitutional act of Congress, and refused to comply with the obligations of the compact when the same are distasteful to the prejudices of their people. As a lawyer, I am prepared to say that parties to such a contract, who have thus violated its provisions when onerous to them, are not entitled to its privileges when demanded by them. And that so long as the "Personal Liberty Bills" disgrace the Statute Books of these States, their electoral votes should not be counted in the Electoral College. But who shall decide upon this question? The Constitution is silent, no provision being made for such a contest. The mode of counting the votes is specified, but no power of decision given to either the Senate or the House, or the General Congress convened. It is an omission in the fundamental law. Who shall decide? The Supreme Court? They have already virtually declared these acts violative of the Constitution, but our opponents and oppressors "spit upon" such decisions. Shall it be decided by force of arms in Washington city? Then civil war must begin there, to end only by the subjugation of one section of the Union. No, my friends, in the absence of any tribunal, the right to decide is one of the "reserved rights" of the States, and Georgia has the privilege of declaring to-day that for herself she decides these votes illegal, and *this election unconstitutional.*

Constitutional Violations

But in another view of this legal question, this man is not chosen as our President. According to the *spirit* of the Constitution, these States have violated its provisions in this election:

First. This Constitution was made for white men—citizens of the United States; this Union was formed by white men, and for the protection and happiness of their race. It is true, that the framers gave to each State the power to declare who should be electors at the ballot-box in each State. But the fair implication was, that this right of suffrage should be given to none but citizens of the United States. Can it be supposed that our fathers intended to allow our national elections to be controlled by men who were not citizens under the National Constitution? Never, never! Yet to elect Abraham Lincoln, the right of suffrage was extended to free negroes in Vermont, Massachusetts, Ohio, New York and other Northern States, although the Supreme Court has declared them not to be citizens of this nation. Yes! Our slaves are first stolen from our midst on underground Railroads, and then voted at Northern ballot-boxes to select rulers for you and me. The memory of our fathers is slandered when this is declared to be according to the Constitution.

Georgia has the privilege of declaring to-day that . . . this election *[is]* unconstitutional.

But, *secondly.* The spirit of the Constitution has been violated in another particular in this election. Ours is a Republican Government, based upon the democratic principle that the majority have a right to rule. That is an anomalous

Government in history or philosophy, which provides for or allows the permanent administration of its powers in the hands of a popular minority. Surely such is not ours. Yet it is true, that counting the unanimous votes of the Southern States and the large minorities in the North against the Black Republicans, a majority amounting to perhaps a million or more votes, have declared against Abraham Lincoln for the next Presidency. Is not this according to the forms of the Constitution? I may be asked. I answer it is. But will my objecting friend answer, is it according to its spirit? I may be told that other Chief Magistrates have been elected by popular minorities. This I admit, but never against such an overwhelming majority, and never by a sectional party based upon the prospect and avowal of a continuation of the same result in every future election. The truth is, that we have lived to see a state of things never contemplated by the framers of the Constitution. At that time we were all slave-holding States—a homogeneous people, having a common origin, common memories—a common cause, common hopes—a common future, a common destiny. The wisdom even of our fathers did not suggest a future when we should be a distinct people, having different social organizations, different pursuits, different memories, different hopes, different destinies. And hence, while the Constitution is full of checks to protect the minority from the sudden and excited power of a majority, no provision was suggested for the protection of the majority from the despotic rule of an infuriated, fanatical, sectional minority. The experience of eight years in the Presidential Chair, and the almost more than human wisdom of Washington gave him a glimpse of the fatal omission thus made in the Constitution, and hence we find in that wonderful document—his Farewell Address—a note of solemn warning against such a perversion of the Government, by the formation of sectional parties. What was thus dimly shadowed to his prophetic ken, is the fact of to-day, and will be history tomorrow. Is it not according to the form of the Constitution? I am asked. I answer it is. Tell me it is in accordance with the spirit and frame work?

Third. The preamble to the Constitution of the United States recites the six leading objects for which it was adopted, namely—"To form a more perfect Union, establish justice, ensure domestic tranquility, provide for the common defense, promote the general welfare, and secure the blessings of liberty to ourselves and our posterity." Had I the time, it would be profitable to take each one of these objects and show how fanaticism had perverted this Government from each and every one of the objects of its organization—how "the Union of hearts and hands," which existed prior to the adoption of the Constitution, had given way to sectional jealousies and mutual hatred—how justice had been denied under the quibbles of executive traitors, outraged both on the bench and in the jury-box—how the common defence had been construed into local advantage, and the general welfare been found in the fleecing of our producers for the fattening of their manufacturers. But these results are not specially attributable to the event we now consider—the election of Lincoln—and hence, I call your attention only to two of these objects—the ensuring of domestic tranquility, and the securing of the blessings of liberty. Recur with me to the parting moment when you left your firesides, to attend upon your public duties at the Capitol. Remember the trembling hand of a loved wife, as she whispered her fears from the incendiary and the assassin. Recall the look of indefinable dread with which the little daughter inquired when your returning footsteps should be heard. And if there be manhood in you, tell me if this is the domestic tranquility which this "glorious Union" has achieved. Notice the anxious look when the travelling pedlar lingers too long in conversation at the door with the servant who turns the bolt—the watchful gaze when the slave tarries long with the wandering artist who professes merely to furnish him with a picture—the suspicion aroused by a Northern man conversing in private with the most faithful of your negroes, and tell me if peace and tranquility are the heritage which this Union has brought to your firesides. Take up your daily papers, and see reports of insurrections in every direction. Hear the telegram read which announces another John Brown raid. Travel on your Railroads and hear, as I did this day, that within seven miles of this Capitol, a gang of slaves have revolted from their labor, declaring themselves free by virtue of Lincoln's election, and say if such fruits as these grow on the good tree of domestic tranquility. Mark me, my friends, I have no fear of any servile insurrection which shall threaten our political existence. Our slaves are the most happy and contented, best fed and best clothed and best paid laboring population in the world, and I would add, also, the *most faithful* and least feared. But a discontented few here and there, will become the incendiary or the poisoner, when instigated by the unscrupulous emissaries of Northern Abolitionists, and you and I cannot say but that your home or your family may be the first to greet your returning footsteps in ashes or in death.—What has given impulse to these fears, and aid and comfort to those outbreaks now, but the success of the Black Republicans—the election of Abraham Lincoln! . . .

We have lived to see a state of things never contemplated by the framers of the Constitution.

Fourth. Equality among the States is the fundamental idea of the American Union. Protection to the life, liberty and property of the citizen is the corner-stone and only end of Government in the American mind. Look to the party whose triumph is to be consummated in the inauguration of Lincoln—The exclusive enjoyment of all the common territory of the Union, is their watchword and party cry. The exclusion of half the States of the Union has been decreed, and we are called upon to record the *fiat* [order]. Will you do it, men of Georgia? Are you so craven so soon? . . .

Time warns me that I cannot pursue this inquiry farther. As a legal question, I am compelled to decide that the election of Lincoln is in violation of the spirit of the Constitution of the United States. And am I told this spirit is too indefinite and shadowy a substance to be made the basis of resistance? And can there be a Georgian who will never resist so long as the form and letter of the Constitution is not broken? Let us inquire. The inter-State Slave Trade is within the letter of the Constitution. Should Congress abolish it will my objector submit? The amendment of the Constitution itself is within the letter of that instrument. If it is so amended in accordance with its letter as to carry out Lincoln's announcement that the States must be all free, will my objector submit? Why not? Because these are violative of its spirit. Truly, my friends, in the words of inspiration, "the letter killeth, but the spirit giveth life." To the spirit then we must look, and a violation of that spirit renders this election unconstitutional.

Dissolution of the Union

I come now to consider this question in its *political* light, and it rises in importance much above the mere legal question.

I must confess that the mere election of a candidate to the Presidency, in a manner legally unconstitutional, does not in my judgment justify necessarily a dissolution of the Union. The wise man and the statesman, to say nothing of the patriot, will always weigh well whether "it is better to bear the ills we have than fly to others that we know not of." And, hence, arises the *political* question, does this election justify and require a disruption of the ties which bind us to the Union? As much as I would dislike the triumph of a purely sectional candidate upon a purely sectional platform, I am free to say I should hesitate even then to risk the consequences of a dissolution, provided that sectional platform *was upon issues not vital in themselves, or were temporary in their nature.* Such, would I conceive to be protective tariffs and homestead bills—the acquisition of territory—peace or war with foreign powers. And if the election of Lincoln, unconstitutional though it may be, was upon a temporary issue, or a question not vital in importance, I should hesitate to declare it ground for Disunion. But my countrymen, I cannot so view the triumph of Black Republicanism. It is a question vital in itself, and by no means, of a temporary character. . .

What has given impulse to these fears, and aid and comfort to those outbreaks now, but the success of the Black Republicans—the election of Abraham Lincoln!

Lincoln and [Senator] Seward spoke the truth when they said, this contest is never ended until all these States are either free or slave. . . .

We have seen, then, that this election is *legally* unconstitutional, and that *politically* the issue on which it is unconstitutional is both *vital* in its importance and *permanent* in its effects. What, then, is our remedy? Shall it be the boy's redress of recrimination? the bully's redress of braggadocio or boasting? or the manly freeman's redress of Independence? This is a most solemn question, and no man should rashly advise his countrymen at such a time. For myself, for months, nay years, I have forseen this coming cloud. I have given it all the study of which my mind is possessed. . . .

Call for Seccesion

Marvel not then that I say my voice is for *immediate, unconditional secession.*

The suggestion for delay comes from various quarters. Good men, and true men, hesitate as to the time. Their counsel deserves attention. Their very doubts are entitled to consideration. . . .

What are their hopes, and on what are they based? I have shown that we cannot expect this fanatical spirit to die, or be appeased. What then shall we look for? From one, I hear the suggestion that perhaps Lincoln may betray his party, and like Fillmore prove to be a conservative. Oh, shame! shame! shame! Is it come to this, that the only hope of Georgia is in the treason of an abolitionist?. . .

Marvel not then that I say my voice is for immediate, unconditional secession.

From another, I hear the suggestion that the Senate can refuse to ratify his appointments, and thus he will be without a cabinet, and without an administration. What is this my friends but revolution and anarchy? We destroy one Government without providing another. And more, and worse, we require our Senators to disregard their oaths to the Constitution, and while within the temple to pull down its pillars. . . .

From another, I hear that we have both Houses of Congress, and hence, Lincoln is powerless. How blindly mistaken! The Executive branch of the Government alone can protect us. The President only can call out the Army and Navy. The President only can appoint Commissioners, and Marshals, and Judges, to execute the Fugitive Slave Law. The President only can protect us from armed invasions and secret incendiaries. . . .

But I am told, suppose Lincoln, in his inaugural, pledges himself to carry out these laws. I would not believe him on his oath. Let them who can trust a Black Republican Abolitionist, hug to their bosom the fatal delusion that we can hope for sweet waters from such a poisoned fountain.

Moreover, why wait for two years when at their close we hope for nothing?. . .

None of these arguments or suggestions carry conviction to my mind. While hope of better things lived, I could be patient and hope on; but when hope died, darkness came, and the only gleam of light in the dark horizon which meets my eye, is from Georgia's star—independent—and if necessary—alone. But we shall not be alone. Our sister on the East [South Carolina] holds out imploring arms to welcome us in our march. Our daughters on the West (Alabama and Mississippi) wait only for their mother to speak. Our neighbor on the South [Florida], to whom just now we are generously yielding a portion of our territory, begs for our counsel and our lead. Georgia, Empire State as she is and deserves to be, must be no laggard in the race. The head of the column is her birthright and her due. To the column's head let us march!

My friends, there is danger in delay. . . .

Delay . . . invites aggression and destroys all confidence in our courage. Let Georgia speak now, and a Northern Regiment will never cross the border line. . . .

Shall I be told to wait for an *overt* act? What act do you expect? What act will be overt? Are not the nullifying Personal Liberty Bills of nine States, *overt?* Are not the daily thefts of our negroes by underground Railroads, *overt?* Are not the national thefts of our national territory, *overt?* Was not the John Brown raid, invading the territory of the South, *overt?* Is not the election of these sectional candidates over a broken Constitution, *overt?* What is the overt act you wish? . . .

My friends, delay is dangerous, for ere long you will be imprisoned by walls of free States all around you. Your increasing slaves will drive out the only race that can move—the whites—and the masters who still cling to their father's graves, will, like the scorpion in a ring of fire, but sting themselves to die. This is your destiny *in the Union. Out of it,* you have a glorious soil—immense natural resources—cotton, the great peace-maker of the world—the best social and political organizations on earth—a people firm, free and independent—the smile of the God we worship illumining our path, and the voice of that God saying, "Occupy till I come."

2

A Pledge to
Uphold the Union

Abraham Lincoln

When he was inaugurated as the sixteenth president of the United States, Abraham Lincoln clearly understood that the country was immersed in the most troubled times of its history. He knew that when he won election in 1860, many in the South were ready to make a clean break from the Union. Indeed, as Lincoln took his oath of office and delivered his inaugural remarks, South Carolina had already seceded; it was only a matter of time before the other Southern states would follow. He also knew that many citizens were looking to him to work a miracle of conciliation and unite the country. In his speech, he affirmed his duty to uphold the Union. He stated his belief—even in light of South Carolina's actions—that, constitutionally, no state could withdraw from the Union.

Fellow Citizens of the United States:
—In compliance with a custom as old as the Government itself, I appear before you to address you briefly, and to take in your presence the oath prescribed by the Constitution of the United States to be taken by the President "before he enters on the execution of his office.". . .

Apprehension seems to exist among the people of the Southern States that by the accession of a Republican administration their property and their peace and personal security are to be endangered. There has never been any reasonable cause for such apprehension. Indeed, the most

Abraham Lincoln, First Inaugural Address, March 4, 1861.

ample evidence to the contrary has all the while existed and been open to their inspection. It is found in nearly all the published speeches of him who now addresses you. I do but quote from one of those speeches when I declare that "I have no purpose, directly or indirectly, to interfere with the institution of slavery in the States where it exists. I believe I have no lawful right to do so, and I have no inclination to do so.". . .

I now reiterate these sentiments; and, in doing so, I only press upon the public attention the most conclusive evidence of which the case is susceptible, that the property, peace and security of no section are to be in any wise endangered by the now incoming administration. I add, too, that all the protection which, consistently with the Constitution and the laws, can be given, will be cheerfully given to all the States when lawfully demanded, for whatever cause—as cheerfully to one section as to another. . . .

I take the official oath to-day with no mental reservations, and with no purpose to construe the Constitution or laws by any hypercritical rules. And, while I do not choose now to specify particular acts of Congress as proper to be enforced, I do suggest that it will be much safer for all, both in official and private stations, to conform to and abide by all those acts which stand unrepealed, than to violate any of them, trusting to find impunity in having them held to be unconstitutional. . . .

A disruption of the Federal Union, heretofore only menaced, is now formidably attempted.

Lincoln's Pledge: Uphold the Union

I hold that, in contemplation of universal law and of the Constitution, the Union of these States is perpetual. Perpetuity is implied, if not expressed, in the fundamental law of all national governments. It is safe to assert that no government proper ever had a provision in its organic law for its own termination. Continue to execute all the express provisions of our national Constitution, and the Union will endure forever—it being impossible to destroy it except by some action not provided for in the instrument itself.

Again, if the United States be not a government proper, but an association of States in the nature of contract merely, can it as a contract be peaceably unmade by less than all the parties who made it? One party to a contract may violate it—break it, so to speak; but does it not require all to law-fully rescind it?

Descending from these general principles, we find the proposition that in legal contemplation the Union is per-petual confirmed by the history of the Union itself. The Union is much older than the Constitution. It was formed, in fact, by the Articles of Association in 1774. It was ma-tured and continued by the Declaration of Independence in 1776. It was further matured, and the faith of all the then thirteen States expressly plighted and engaged that it should be perpetual, by the Articles of Confederation in 1778. And, finally, in 1787 one of the declared objects for ordaining and establishing the Constitution was "to form a more perfect Union."

I have no purpose, directly or indirectly, to interfere with the institution of slavery in the States where it exists.

But if the destruction of the Union by one or by a part only of the States be lawfully possible, the Union is less per-fect than before the Constitution, having lost the vital ele-ment of perpetuity.

It follows from these views that no State upon its own mere motion can lawfully get out of the Union; that resolves and ordinances to that effect are legally void; and that acts of violence, within any State or States, against the authority of the United States, are insurrectionary or revolutionary, according to circumstances.

I therefore consider that, in view of the Constitution and the laws, the Union is unbroken; and to the extent of my ability I shall take care, as the Constitution itself ex-pressly enjoins upon me, that the laws of the Union be faith-fully executed in all the States. Doing this I deem to be only a simple duty on my part; and I shall perform it so far as practicable, unless my rightful masters, the American people, shall withhold the requisite means, or in some au-thoritative manner direct the contrary. I trust this will not be regarded as a menace, but only as the declared purpose of the Union that it will constitutionally defend and main-tain itself.

In doing this there needs to be no bloodshed or violence; and there shall be none, unless it be forced upon the national authority. The power confided to me will be used to hold, occupy, and possess the property and places belonging to the Government, and to collect the duties and imposts; but beyond what may be necessary for these objects, there will be no invasion, no using of force against or among the people anywhere. Where hostility to the United States, in any interior locality, shall be so great and universal as to prevent competent resident citizens from holding the Federal offices, there will be no attempt to force obnoxious strangers among the people for that object. While the strict legal right may exist in the government to enforce the exercise of these offices, the attempt to do so would be so irritating, and so nearly impracticable withal, that I deem it better to forego for the time the uses of such offices.

Abraham Lincoln

The mails, unless repelled, will continue to be furnished in all parts of the Union. So far as possible, the people everywhere shall have that sense of perfect security which is most favorable to calm thought and reflection. The course here indicated will be followed unless current events and experience shall show a modification or change to be proper, and in every case and exigency my best discretion will be exercised according to circumstances actually existing, and with a view and a hope of a peaceful solution of the national troubles and the restoration of fraternal sympathies and affections.

That there are persons in one section or another who seek to destroy the Union at all events, and are glad of any pretext to do it, I will neither affirm nor deny; but if there be such, I need address no word to them. To those, however, who really love the Union may I not speak?

The Question of Secession

Before entering upon so grave a matter as the destruction of our national fabric, with all its benefits, its memories, and its hopes, would it not be wise to ascertain precisely why we do it? Will you hazard so desperate a step while there is any possibility that any portion of the ills you fly from have no real existence? Will you, while the certain ills you fly to are greater than all the real ones you fly from—will you risk the commission of so fearful a mistake?

All profess to be content in the Union if all constitutional rights can be maintained. Is it true, then, that any right, plainly written in the Constitution, has been denied? I think not. . . .

Shall fugitives from labor be surrendered by national or by State authority? The Constitution does not expressly say. May Congress protect slavery in the Territories? The Constitution does not expressly say. Must Congress protect slavery in the Territories? The Constitution does not expressly say.

From questions of this class spring all our constitutional controversies, and we divide upon them into majorities and minorities. If the minority will not acquiesce, the majority must, or the Government must cease. There is no other alternative; for continuing the Government is acquiescence on one side or the other.

There will be no invasion, no using of force against or among the people anywhere.

If a minority in such a case will secede rather than acquiesce, they make a precedent which in turn will divide and ruin them; for a minority of their own will secede from them whenever a majority refuses to be controlled by such minority. For instance, why may not any portion of a new confederacy a year or two hence arbitrarily secede again, precisely as portions of the present Union now claim to secede from it? All who cherish disunion sentiments are now being educated to the exact temper of doing this.

Is there such perfect identity of interests among the States to compose a new Union as to produce harmony only, and prevent renewed secession?

Plainly, the central idea of secession is the essence of anarchy. A majority held in restraint by constitutional checks and limitations, and always changing easily with deliberate changes of popular opinions and sentiments, is the only true sovereign of a free people. Whoever rejects it does, of necessity, fly to anarchy or to despotism. Unanimity is impossible; the rule of a minority, as a permanent arrangement, is wholly inadmissible; so that, rejecting the majority principle, anarchy or despotism in some form is all that is left. . . .

One section of our country believes slavery is right, and ought to be extended, while the other believes it is wrong, and ought not to be extended. This is the only substantial dispute. The fugitive slave clause of the Constitution and the law for the suppression of the foreign slave trade are each as well enforced, perhaps, as any law can ever be in a community where the moral sense of the people imperfectly supports the law itself. The great body of the people abide by the dry legal obligation in both cases, and a few break over in each. This, I think, cannot be perfectly cured; and it would be worse in both cases after the separation of the sections than before. The foreign slave trade, now imperfectly suppressed, would be ultimately revived, without restriction, in one section, while fugitive slaves, now only partially surrendered, would not be surrendered at all by the other.

Physically speaking, we cannot separate. We cannot remove our respective sections from each other, nor build an impassable wall between them. A husband and wife may be divorced and go out of the presence and beyond the reach of each other; but the different parts of our country cannot do this. They cannot but remain face to face, and intercourse, either amicable or hostile, must continue between them. Is it possible, then, to make that intercourse more advantageous or more satisfactory after separation than before? Can aliens make treaties easier than friends can make laws? Can treaties be more faithfully enforced between aliens than laws can among friends? Suppose you go to war, you cannot fight always; and when, after much loss on both sides, and no gain on either, you cease fighting, the identical old questions as to terms of intercourse are again upon you.

Physically speaking, we cannot separate.

This country, with its institutions, belongs to the people who inhabit it. Whenever they shall grow weary of the existing government, they can exercise their constitutional right of amending it, or their revolutionary right to dismember or overthrow it. I cannot be ignorant of the fact that many worthy and patriotic citizens are desirous of having the national Constitution amended. While I make no recommendation of amendments, I fully recognize the rightful authority of the people over the whole subject, to be exercised in either of the modes prescribed in the instrument itself, and I should, under existing circumstances, favor rather than oppose a fair opportunity being afforded the people to act upon it. I will venture to add that to me the convention mode seems preferable, in that it allows amendments to originate with the people themselves, instead of only permitting them to take or reject propositions originated by others not especially chosen for the purpose, and which might not be precisely such as they would wish to either accept or refuse. I understand a proposed amendment to the Constitution—which amendment, however, I have not seen—has passed Congress, to the effect that the Federal Government shall never interfere with the domestic institutions of the States, including that of persons held to service. To avoid misconstruction of what I have said, I depart from my purpose not to speak of particular amendments so far as to say that, holding such a provision to now be implied constitutional law, I have no objection to its being made express and irrevocable. . . .

Justice Will Prevail

Why should there not be a patient confidence in the ultimate justice of the people? Is there any better or equal hope in the world? In our present differences is either party without faith of being in the right? If the Almighty Ruler of nations, with his eternal truth and justice, be on your side of the North, or on yours of the South, that truth and that justice will surely prevail by the judgment of this great tribunal of the American people.

By the frame of the government under which we live, this same people have wisely given their public servants but little power for mischief; and have, with equal wisdom, provided for the return of that little to their own hands at very short intervals. While the people retain their virtue and vigilance, no administration, by any extreme of wickedness or folly, can very seriously injure the government in the short space of four years.

My countrymen, one and all, think calmly and well

upon this whole subject. Nothing valuable can be lost by taking time. If there be an object to hurry any of you in hot haste to a step which you would never take deliberately, that object will be frustrated by taking time; but no good object can be frustrated by it. Such of you as are now dissatisfied still have the old Constitution unimpaired, and, on the sensitive point, the laws of your own framing under it; while the new administration will have no immediate power, if it would, to change either. If it were admitted that you who are dissatisfied hold the right side in the dispute, there still is no single good reason for precipitate action. Intelligence, patriotism, Christianity, and a firm reliance on Him who has never yet forsaken this favored land, are still competent to adjust in the best way all our present difficulty.

In your hands, my dissatisfied fellow countrymen, and not in mine, is the momentous issue of civil war. The government will not assail you. You can have no conflict without being yourselves the aggressors. You have no oath registered in heaven to destroy the government, while I shall have the most solemn one to "preserve, protect, and defend" it.

I am loath to close. We are not enemies, but friends. We must not be enemies. Though passion may have strained, it must not break, our bonds of affection. The mystic chords of memory, stretching from every battle-field and patriot grave to every living heart and hearthstone all over this broad land, will yet swell the chorus of the Union when again touched, as surely they will be, by the better angels of our nature.

3

Only by Acknowledging the Right to Secede Can War Be Prevented

Judah P. Benjamin

By 1860, the United States was embroiled in a crisis, and the issue of slavery was at the center of this crisis. Talk of secession and of war filled the halls of both state and federal governments. The Southern states viewed the ability to maintain the institution of slavery within their borders as their sovereign right. It was not a moral question: Any encroachment upon that sovereign right would mean an end to their agrarian economy and their way of life. With secession increasingly viewed as the only means to end the crisis within the Union, South Carolina became the first of the Southern states to secede. In response to South Carolina's secession, Senator Judah P. Benjamin addressed the Senate floor. In his speech, he encouraged his fellow senators to recognize South Carolina's claim to independence and the right of any of the other Southern states to exercise their right to self-government and secede from the Union. Only then, he argued, could the prospect of war be averted and peace between the states be maintained.

When I took the floor at our last adjournment, I stated that I expected to address the Senate to-day in reference to the critical issue now before the country. I had supposed that by this time there would have been some official communications to the Senate, in reference to the fact now

Judah P. Benjamin, speech before the United States Senate, December 31, 1860.

known to all, of the condition of affairs in South Carolina. I will assume, for purposes of the remarks that I have to make, that those facts have been officially communicated, and address myself to them. Probably never had a deliberative assembly been called upon to determine questions calculated to awaken a more solemn sense of responsibility than those that now address themselves to our consideration. We are brought at last sir, directly forced, to meet promptly an issue produced by an irresistible course of events whose inevitable results some of us, at least, have foreseen for years. Nor, sir, have we failed in our duty of warning the Republicans that they were fast driving us to a point where the very instincts of self-preservation would impose upon us the necessity of separation. We repeated those warnings with a depth of conviction, with an earnestness of assertion that inspired the hope that we should succeed in imparting at least some faint assurance of our sincerity to those by whose aid alone could the crisis be averted. But, sir, our assertions were derided, our predictions were scoffed at; all our honest and patriotic efforts to save the Constitution and the Union sneered at and maligned, as dictated, not by love of country, but by base ambition for place and power. . . .

South Carolina's Secession

Alas, the feelings and sentiments expressed since the commencement of this session, on the opposite side of this floor, almost force the belief that a civil war is their desire; and that the day is full near when American citizens are to meet each other in hostile array; and when the hands of brothers will be reddened with the blood of brothers.

The State of South Carolina, with a unanimity scarcely with parallel in history, has dissolved the union which connects her with the other States of the confederacy, and declared herself independent. We, the representatives of those remaining States, stand here to-day, bound either to recognize that independence, or to overthrow it; either to permit her peaceful secession from the confederacy, or to put her down by force of arms. That is the issue. That is the sole issue. No artifice from an excited or alarmed public, can suffice to conceal it. Those attempts are equally futile and disingenuous. As for the attempted distinction between coercing a State, and forcing all the people of the State, by arms, to yield obedience to an authority repudiated by the sovereign will of the State, expressed in its most authentic form, it is as unsound in principle as it is impossible of practical application. Upon that point, however, I shall have something to say a little further on.

If we elevate ourselves to the height from which we are bound to look in order to embrace all the vast consequence that must result from our decision, we are not permitted to ignore the fact that our determination does not involve the State of South Carolina alone. Next week, Mississippi, Alabama, and Florida, will have declared themselves independent; the week after, Georgia; and a little later, Louisiana; soon, very soon, to be followed by Texas and Arkansas. I confine myself purposely to these eight States, because I wish to speak only of those whose action we know with positive certainty, and which no man can for a moment pretend to controvert. I designedly exclude others, about whose action I feel equally confident, although others may raise a cavil.

The Right to Secede

Shall we recognize the fact that South Carolina has become an independent State, or shall we wage war against her! And first as to her right. I do not agree with those who think it idle to discuss that right. . . .

From the time that this people declared its independence of Great Britain, the right of the people to self-government in its fullest and broadest extent has been a cardinal principle of American liberty. None deny it. And in that right, to use the language of the Declaration itself, is included the right whenever a form of government becomes destructive of their interests or their safety, "to alter or to abolish it, and to institute a new government, laying its foundation on such principles and organizing its powers in such form as to them shall seem most likely to effect their safety and happiness.". . .

I say . . . that the right of the people of one generation, in convention duly assembled, to alter the institutions bequeathed by their fathers is inherent, inalienable, not susceptible of restriction; that by the same power under which one Legislature can repeal the act of a former Legislature, so can one convention of the people duly assembled; and that it is in strict and logical deduction from this fundamental principle of American liberty, that South Carolina has adopted the form in which she has declared her independence. She has in convention duly assembled in 1860, repealed an ordinance passed by her people in convention duly assembled in 1788. . . .

These States, parties to the compact, have a right to withdraw from it, by virtue of its own provisions are violated by the other parties to the compact, when either powers not granted are usurped, or rights are refused that are especially granted to the States. But there is a large class of powers granted by this Constitution, in the exercise of which a discretion these admitted powers might be so perverted and abused as to give cause of complaint, and, finally, to give the right to revolution; for under those circumstances there would be no other remedy. . . .

We stand here to-day, bound . . . either to permit her peaceful secession from the confederacy, or to put her down by force of arms.

I say, therefore, that I distinguish the rights of the States under the Constitution into two classes; on resulting from the nature of their bargain; if the bargain is broken by the sister States, to consider themselves freed from it on the ground of breach of compact; if the bargain be not broken, but the powers be perverted to their wrong and their oppression, then, whenever that wrong and oppression shall become sufficiently aggravated, the revolutionary right— the last inherent right of man to preserve freedom, property, and safety—arises, and must be exercised, for none other will meet the case.

War or Peace

But suppose South Carolina to be altogether wrong in her opinion that this compact has been violated to her prejudice, and that she has, therefore, a right to withdraw; take that for granted—what then? You will have the same issue to meet, face to face. You must permit her to withdraw in peace, or you must declare war. That is, you must coerce the State itself, or you must permit her to depart in peace. . . .

We cannot go to war; we are not going to war; we are not going to coerce a State. "Why," says the Senator from Illinois, "who talks of coercing a State: you are attempting to breed confusion in the public mind; you are attempting to impose upon people by perverting the question; we only mean to execute the laws against individuals." Again, I say, where will be the civil process which must precede the action of the military force? Surely, surely it is not at this day that we are to argue that neither the President, nor the President and Congress combined, are armed with the powers of a military despot to carry out the laws, without the intervention of the courts, according to their own caprice and their own discretion, to judge when laws are violated, to convict for the violation, to pronounce sentence, and to execute it. You can do nothing of the kind with your military force. . . .

This whole scheme, this whole fancy, that you can treat the act of sovereign State, issued in an authoritative form, and in her collective capacity as a State, as being utterly out of existence; that you can treat the State as still belonging collectively to the Confederacy, and that you can proceed, without a solitary Federal officer in the State, to enforce your laws against private individuals, is as vain, as idle, and delusive as any dream that ever entered into the head of man. The thing cannot be done. It is only asserted for the purpose of covering up the true question, than which there is no other; you must acknowledge the independence of the seceding State, or reduce her to subjection by war.

The right of the people to self-government . . . has been a cardinal principle of American liberty.

I desire not to enter in any detail into the dreary catalogue of wrongs and outrages by which South Carolina defends the position that she has withdrawn from this Union because she has a constitutional right to do so, by reason of prior violations of the compact by her sister States. Before, however, making any statement—that statement to which we have been challenged, and which I shall make in but very few words—of the wrongs under which the South is now suffering, and for which she seeks redress, as the difficulty seems to arise chiefly from a difference in our construction of the Constitution. . . .

You, Senators of the Republican party, assert, and your people whom you represent assert, that under a just and fair interpretation of the Federal Constitution it is right that you deny that our slaves, which directly and indirectly involve a value of more than four thousand million dollars, are property at all, or entitled to protection in Territories owned by the common Government.

You assume the interpretation that it is right to encourage, by all possible means, directly or indirectly, the robbery of this property, and to legislate so as to render its recovery as difficult and dangerous as possible; that it is right and proper and justifiable, under the Constitution, to prevent our mere transit across a sister State, to embark with our property on a lawful voyage, without being openly despoiled of it.

You assert, and practice upon the assertion, that it is right to hold us up to the ban of mankind, in speech, writing, and print, with every appliance of publicity, as thieves, robbers, murderers, villains, and criminals of the blackest dye, because we continue to own property which we owned at the time we all signed the compact.

That it is right that we should be exposed to spend our treasure in the purchase, or shed our blood in the conquest, of foreign territory, with no right to enter it for settlement without leaving behind our most valuable property, under penalty of its confiscation.

You practically interpret this instrument to be that it is eminently in accordance with the assurance that our tranquility and welfare were to be preserved and promoted, that our sister States should combine to prevent our growth and development; that they should surround us with a cordon of hostile communities, for the express and avowed purpose of accumulating in dense masses, and within restricted limits, a population which you believe to be dangerous, and thereby force the sacrifice of property nearly sufficient in value to pay the public debt of every nation in Europe.

We cannot go to war; we are not going to war.

This is the construction of the instrument that was to preserve our security, promote our welfare, and which we only signed on your assurance that that was its object. You tell us that this is a fair construction—not all of you, some say one thing, some another; but you act, or your people do, upon this principle. You do not propose to enter into our

States, you say, and what do we complain of? You do not pretend to enter into our States to kill or destroy our institution by force. Oh, no. You imitate the faith of Rhadamistus: you propose simply to close us in an embrace that will suffocate us. You do not propose to fell the tree; you promise not. You merely propose to girdle it, that it die. And then, when we tell you that we do not understand this bargain this way, that your acting upon it in this spirit releases us for the obligation that accompany it; that under no circumstances can we consent to live together under the interpretation, and say: "we will go from you; let us go in peace"; we are answered by your leading spokesmen: "Oh, no; you cannot do that.". . .

Let this parting be in peace.

Now, Senators, this picture is not placed before you with any idea that it will act upon any one of you, or change your views, or alter your conduct. All hope of that is gone. Our committee has reported this morning that no possible scheme of adjustment can be devised by them all combined. The day for the adjustment has passed. If you would give it now, you are too late.

And now, Senators, within a few weeks we part to meet as Senators in one common council chamber of the nation no more forever. We desire, we beseech you, let this parting be in peace. I conjure you to indulge in no vain delusion that duty or conscience, interest or honor, impose upon you the necessity of invading our States or shedding the blood of our people. You have no possible justification for it. I trust it is in no craven spirit, and with no sacrifice of the honor or dignity of my own State, that I make this last appeal, but from far higher and holier motives. If, however, it shall prove vain, if you are resolved to pervert the Government framed by the fathers for the protection of our rights into an instrument for subjugating and enslaving us, then, appealing to the Supreme Judge of the universe for the rectitude of our intention, we must meet the issue that you force upon us as best becomes freemen defending all that is dear to man.

What may be the fate of this horrible contest, no man can tell, none pretend to foresee; but this much I will say: the fortunes of war may be adverse to our arms; you may carry desolation into our peaceful land, and with torch and fire you may set our cities in flames; you may even emulate the atrocities of those who, in the war of the revolution, hounded on the blood-thirsty savage to attack upon the defenseless frontier; you may, under the protection of your advancing armies, give shelter to the furious fanatics who desire, and profess to desire, nothing more than to add all the horrors of a servile insurrection to the calamities of civil war; you may do all this—and more, too, if more there be—but you never can subjugate us; you never can convert the free sons of the soil into vassals, paying tribute to your power; and you never, never can degrade them to the level of an inferior and servile race. Never! Never!

4

There Is No Right
to Secede

Boston *Daily Atlas and Bee*

Northerners often seemed not to hear the South's impassioned cry for sovereignty and the right to secede. To many in the North, secession was a nonissue because people there firmly believed that no state had the right to secede. In the excerpts that follow, Boston editorial writers decry any right on the part of Southerners to secede, because the federal government has not interfered with any of their rights to self-government. The editors also emphatically assert that the Southern states have neither the power nor the economic viability to separate from the Union. But, even if these Southern states did wield such power, these writers state confidently, the executive, legislative, and judicial branches of the Union would never allow such a break to occur.

The most prominent, and indeed almost the only topic of political interest just now, is the rumored insane attempt of a few hot-headed fanatics, to induce the people of a few slave States to secede from the American Union. There is in this nothing new, unexpected, or alarming. The truth is, the slave States have neither the right, the power, nor the inclination to secede—therefore they will not. Let us consider the matter a little. The right of a sovereign confederated State to withdraw has been often asserted, and is now believed in by many men both South and North; but it has been generally denied, and the arguments in its favor controverted by all the ablest statesmen and patriots of the coun-

Boston Daily Atlas and Bee, "Editorial," *Daily Atlas and Bee*, November 12, 1860.

try. [Congressman Daniel] . . . Webster's argument against the right of secession is, in our judgment, unanswerable, and we suggest to those who think the right of secession defensible, a perusal of that great statesman's opinion. So long as the several States retain, as they now do, sovereign control, within their own domain, of all their local affairs, and are not interfered with by the federal authorities in those State concerns, it is absurd to claim the right of secession. Those concerns that are committed to the exclusive jurisdiction and control of the federal government, were so committed by the original confederated States, with the distinct understanding that the States should not attempt to resume these delegated powers. They have no more right to claim the rendering back to them of these federal prerogatives, than the general government has to claim any control over subjects of special and exclusive State jurisdiction.

No Right to Secede

In only one conceivable contingency could the right to secede be maintained, and that goes back to the primal right of revolution, of rebellion against an existing government. Should the federal government undertake to take away from a State the control of its State affairs, within its State jurisdiction, then a State might claim the right of revolutionary resistance, on the ground that the federal government had itself violated the compact and rendered it null and void. But no man pretends that any such case as this has arisen, or is likely to arise. The rights of no State have been interfered with by the federal government, nor is there any purpose, declared or supposed, on the part of the present or the incoming administration to give any such provocation to rebellion. If it be said that the right of some States have been interfered with by other States, acting in their separate capacity of State sovereignty, this although true would not meet the case nor afford any basis for revolution. A law of Massachusetts may be oppressive of a citizen of South Carolina, but even if so, it is operative only within Massachusetts domain and jurisdiction. Exactly so with the laws of South Carolina, which are unjust towards citizens of Massachusetts. Besides, if there are cases of this sort in one section of the country, there are as many and as flagrant in the other, and the only defensible mode of redress or adjustment is through the arbitration of Congress and the judicial tribunals of the country.

If the federal government should attempt to invade the domain of State rights, that would be despotism and cause of resistance—but there is no such cause, and there will be none. Should any State attempt to resume powers expressly yielded to the federal government, that would be treason, and would justify the exercise of forcible means by the federal government to bring back the offending State to its allegiance to the Constitution and the Union. But no such case has arisen—none will arise. There is, therefore, no existing right of secession, and the claim for it is utterly indefensible. Secession ought not to be, and that is one of the strongest reasons why it never will be.

Slave States Lack the Power

Secondly, the slave States have not the power to secede. Unless permitted by the federal government quietly to withdraw, they cannot go. It is absurd to suppose that a President and a Congress and a Judiciary sworn to maintain the Constitution and the laws will ever permit a State to secede. If they should, they would violate their oaths and become participants in the crime of treason. The only other possible method of secession is by violence, involving the nullification of the federal laws and armed resistance to the federal authority. In such a contest the slave States would be speedily and deservedly crushed by the strong arm of power. They have neither the wealth, the intelligence, the arts, the arms, nor the character, requisite to maintain the struggle.

The truth is, the slave States have neither the right, the power, nor the inclination to secede.

The preponderance of all these elements of power is so largely with those States that will remain loyal to the confederacy, as to render the idea of the ability of the slave States to secede utterly preposterous. The only results to the rebellious States would be a bloody strife confined entirely to their own territory, the immediate and violent abolition of slavery, the destruction of their commerce, the ruin of all their material interests and finally a forced submission to the authority they had resisted and the government they had defied. This we say in no spirit of unkindness or boasting, but because these are the incontrovertible facts which no appeals of passion or flourishes of rhetoric can remove or change.

Slave States Lack the Desire

Thirdly, the slave States have no inclination to secede. A reckless and passionate minority, a very small minority, of the people of three or four States are preaching disunion. But they are all either intriguing politicians or are adventurers, who are playing upon the fears of the people and raising an uproar in Ephesus because "their craft is in danger." They see in the accession of the Republican party to power the certain end of that reign of terrorism over the expression of public opinion at the South, by means of which they have so long climbed to places of political power and exercised a domination in the federal government.

They are not in the least apprehensive of the abolition of slavery, or of any aggression upon southern rights by the administration of Abraham Lincoln; but they do apprehend and with good reason that their political ascendancy in the South is about to terminate, and that power there will soon pass into the hands of the patriotic, liberty-loving men of that section of the country. . . .

The great mass of the southern people desire no secession or disunion; they are loyal to the government, patriotic in their feelings, and laugh to scorn the treason and the nonsense of the braggarts and demagogues with whose presence and blatant bellowings they are now afflicted. Nobody in the free States need feel any anxiety about secession. The people of the South will take care of these agitators— if they don't, Old Abe will. If ever any actual attempt is made to subvert the Constitution or destroy the Union, if any assault is made upon the integrity of the Republic by fanatics from any section or party, the law-abiding, loyal and patriotic men of the slave States will stand as a wall of fire against them, and will meet and roll back their turbulent hosts, as the solid cliffs of the ocean shore beat back the angry surges of the sea.

Such is our judgment of the prospect and the probability of secession and disunion; and until philosophy is false, experience vain, reason powerless, facts converted into fiction, self-interest no longer the main-spring of human action, and principle extinct, that judgment will be vindicated and verified by the events of the future.

5

The Union Must Prevail

Andrew Johnson

In the years before the Civil War, mounting tension arose between two camps. On the one hand were those who upheld as paramount the rule of law of the U.S. Constitution and the existence of the country as a *union* of states; on the other were those who upheld the rights of the states to govern themselves and override any federal mandates. To those who believed in the principal importance of the rule of the federal government, a strong union represented America's ability to move forward with a coherent national vision. It also represented the strength to marshal military and economic forces as needed for the public good. Although he was from the South, Tennessee senator Andrew Johnson had strong sentiments about the importance of maintaining the Union in the midst of the secession crisis. In a speech before the U.S. Senate, excerpted below, Johnson stated emphatically that no state had the power to withdraw from the Union. He felt that any disagreements with the federal government could be handled within the Union and within the framework of the Constitution. In addition, he argued that if states could secede at will, the federal government "and the guarantees under which this Union has grown" did not have long to exist.

I think it behooves every man, and especially every one occupying a public place, to indicate, in some manner, his opinions and sentiments in reference to the questions that agitate and distract the public mind. I shall be frank on this occasion in giving my views and taking my positions, as I have always been upon questions that involve the public in-

Andrew Johnson, speech before the United States Senate, December 18, 1860.

terest. I believe it is the imperative duty of Congress to make some effort to save the country from impending dissolution; and he that is unwilling to make an effort to preserve the Union, or, in other words, to preserve the Constitution, and the Union as an incident resulting from the preservation of the Constitution, I think is unworthy of public confidence, and the respect and gratitude of the American people. I say it devolves upon every one who can contribute in the slightest degree to this result to come forward and make some effort, reasonable in its character, to preserve the Union of these States by a preservation of the Constitution.

Opposed to Secession

In most that I shall say on this occasion, I shall not differ very essentially from my southern friends. The difference will consist, as I think, from what I have heard and what I see published in the various periodicals of the day, in the mode and manner by which this great end is to be accomplished. Some of our southern friends think that secession is the mode by which these ends can be accomplished; that if the Union cannot be preserved in its spirit, by secession they will get those rights secured and perpetuated that they have failed to obtain within the Union. I am opposed to secession. I believe it is no remedy for the evils complained of. Instead of acting with that division of my southern friends who take ground for secession, I shall take other grounds while I try to accomplish the same end.

I think that this battle ought to be fought not outside, but inside of the Union, and upon the battlements of the Constitution itself. I am unwilling, of my own volition, to walk outside of the Union which has been the result of a Constitution made by the patriots of the Revolution. They formed the Constitution; and this Union that is so much spoken of, and which all of us are so desirous to preserve, grows out of the Constitution; and I repeat, I am not willing to walk out of the Union growing out of the Constitution, that was formed by the patriots and, I may say, the soldiers of the Revolution. So far as I am concerned, and I believe I may speak with some degree of confidence for the people of my State, we intend to fight that battle inside and not outside of the Union; and if anybody must go out of the Union, it must be those who violate it. We do not intend to go out. It is our Constitution; it is our Union, growing out of the Constitution; and we do not intend to be driven from it or out of the Union. Those who have violated the Constitution either in the passage of what are denominated personal liberty bills, or by their refusal to execute the fugitive slave law—they having violated the instrument that binds us together—must go out and not we. I do not think we can go before the country with the same force of position demanding of the North a compliance with the Constitution and all its guarantees, if we violate the Constitution by going out ourselves, that we shall if we stand inside of the Constitution, and demand a compliance with its provisions and guarantees; or if need be, as I think it is, to demand additional securities. We should make that demand inside of the Constitution, and in the manner and mode pointed out by the instrument itself. Then we keep ourselves in the right; we put our adversary in the wrong; and though it may take a little longer to accomplish the end, we take the right means to accomplish an end that is right in itself.

It is the imperative duty of Congress to make some effort to save the country from impending dissolution.

I know that sometimes we talk about compromises. I am not a compromiser, nor a conservative, in the usual acceptation of those terms. I have been generally considered radical, and I do not come forward today in anything that I shall say or propose, asking anything to be done upon the principle of compromise. If we ask for anything, it should be for that which is right and reasonable in itself. It being right, those of whom we ask it, upon the great principle of right, are bound to grant it. Compromise! I know in the common acceptance of the term it is to agree upon certain propositions in which some things are conceded on one side and others conceded on the other. I shall go for enactments by Congress or for amendments to the Constitution, upon the principle that they are right and upon no other ground. I am not for compromising right with wrong. If we have no right, we ought not to demand it. If we are in the wrong, they should not grant us what we ask. I approach this momentous subject on the great principles of right, asking nothing and demanding nothing but what is right in itself and which every right-minded man and a right-minded community and a right-minded people, who wish the preservation of this Government, will be disposed to grant.

We deny that a State has the power, of its own volition, to withdraw from the Confederacy.

In fighting this battle, I shall do it upon the basis laid down by a portion of the people of my own State, in a large and very intelligent meeting. A committee of the most intelligent men in the country reported, in the shape of resolutions, to this meeting the basis upon which I intend to fight this great battle for our rights. They reported this resolution:

> *Resolved*, That we deeply sympathize with our sister southern States, and freely admit that there is good cause for dissatisfaction and complaint on their part, on account of the recent election of sectional candidates to the Presidency and Vice Presidency of the United States; yet we, as a portion of the people of a slave-holding community, are not for seceding or breaking up the union of these States until every fair and honorable means has been exhausted in trying to obtain, on the part of the non-slaveholding States, a compliance with the spirit and letter of the Constitution and all its guarantees; and when this shall have been done, and the States now in open rebellion against the laws of the United States, in refusing to execute the fugitive slave law, shall persist in their present unconstitutional course, and the Federal Government shall fail or refuse to execute the laws in good faith, it (the Government) will not have accomplished the great design of its creation, and will therefore, in fact, be a practical dissolution, and all the States, as parties, be released from the compact which formed the Union.

The people of Tennessee, irrespective of party, go on and declare further:

> That in the opinion of this meeting no State has the constitutional right to secede from the Union without the consent of the other States which ratified the compact. The compact, when ratified, formed the Union

without making any provision whatever for its dissolution. It (the compact) was adopted by the States *in toto and forever, 'without reservation or condition;'* hence a secession of one or more States from the Union, without the consent of the others ratifying the compact, would be revolution, leading in the end to civil, and perhaps servile war. While we deny the right of a State, constitutionally, to secede from the Union, we admit the great and inherent right of revolution, abiding and remaining with every people, but a right which should not be exercised, except in extreme cases, and in the last resort, when grievances are without redress, and oppression has become intolerable.

They declare further:

That in our opinion, we can more successfully resist the aggression of Black Republicanism by remaining within the Union, than we can by going out of it; and more especially so, while there is a majority of both branches in the National Legislature opposed to it, and the Supreme Court of the United States is on the side of law and the Constitution.

They go on, and declare further:

That we are not willing to abandon our northern friends who have stood by the Constitution of the United States, and in standing by it have vindicated our rights, and in their vindication have been struck down; and now, in their extremity, we cannot and will not desert them by seceding, or otherwise breaking up the Union.

This is the basis upon which a portion of the people of Tennessee, irrespective of party, propose to fight this battle. We believe that our true position is inside of the Union. We deny the doctrine of secession; we deny that a State has the power, of its own volition, to withdraw from the Confederacy. We are not willing to do an unconstitutional act, to induce or to coerce others to comply with the Constitution of the United States. We prefer complying with the Constitution and fighting our battle, and making our demand inside of the Union.

I know, Mr. President, that there are some who believe—

and we see that some of the States are acting on that principle—that a State has the right to secede; that, of its own will, it has a right to withdraw from the Confederacy. . . .

This doctrine of a State, either assuming her highest political attitude or otherwise, having the right of her own will to dissolve all connection with this Confederacy, is an absurdity, and contrary to the plain intent and meaning of the Constitution of the United States. I hold that the Constitution of the United States makes no provision, as said by the President of the United States, for its own destruction. It makes no provision for breaking up the Government, and no State has the constitutional right to secede and withdraw from the Union. . . .

Avenues of Redress

I know that the inquiry may be made, how is a State, then, to have redress? There is but one way, and that is expressed by the people of Tennessee. You have entered into this compact; it was mutual; it was reciprocal; and of your own volition have no right to withdraw and break the compact, without the consent of the other parties. What remedy, then, has the State? It has a remedy that remains and abides with every people upon the face of the earth—when grievances are without a remedy, or without redress, when oppression becomes intolerable, they have the great inherent right of revolution, and that is all there is of it.

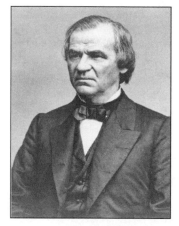

Sir, if the doctrine of secession is to be carried out upon the mere whim of a State, this Government is at an end. I am as much opposed to a strong, or what may be called by some a consolidated Government, as it is possible for a man to be;

Andrew Johnson

but while I am greatly opposed to that, I want a Government strong enough to preserve its own existence; that will not fall to pieces by its own weight or whenever a little dissatisfaction takes place in one of its members. If the States have the right to secede at will and pleasure, for real or imaginary evils or oppressions, I repeat again, this Government is at an end; it is not stronger than a rope of sand; its own weight will tumble it to pieces and it cannot exist. Notwithstanding this doctrine may suit some who are engaged in this perilous and impending crisis that is now upon us, duty to my country, duty to my State, and duty to my kind, require me to avow a doctrine that I believe will result in the preservation of the Government, and to repudiate one that I believe will result in its overthrow, and the consequent disasters to the people of the United States.

If a State can secede at will and pleasure, and this doctrine is maintained, why, I ask, on the other hand, and as Mr. Madison argues in one of his letters, cannot a majority of the States combine and reject a State out of the Confederacy? Have a majority of these States, under the compact they have made with each other, the right to combine and reject any one of the States from the Confederacy? They have no such right; the compact is reciprocal. It was ratified without reservation or condition, and it was ratified "*in toto* and forever;" such is the language of James Madison; and there is but one way to get out of it without the consent of the parties, and that is, by revolution.

I want a Government strong enough to preserve its own existence.

I know that some touch on the subject with trembling and fear. They say, here is a State that, perhaps by this time, has seceded, or if not, she is on the road to secession, and we must touch this subject very delicately; and that if the State secedes, conceding the power of the Constitution to her to secede, you must talk very delicately upon the subject of coercion. I do not believe the Federal Government has the power to coerce a State; for by the eleventh amendment of the Constitution of the United States it is expressly provided that you cannot even put one of the States of this Confederacy before one of the courts of the country as a party. As a State, the Federal Government has no power to coerce it; but it is a member of the compact to which it agreed in common with the other States, and this Government has the right to pass laws, and to enforce those laws upon individuals within the limits of each State. While the one proposition is clear, the other is equally so. This Government can, by the Constitution of the country and by the laws enacted in conformity with the Constitution, operate upon individuals, and has the right and the power, not to coerce a State, but to enforce and execute the law upon individuals within the limits of a State.

I know the term, "to coerce a State," is used in an *ad captandum* manner. It is a sovereignty that is to be crushed! How is a State in the Union? What is her connection with it? All the connection she has with the other States is that which is agreed upon in the compact between the States. I do not know whether you may consider it in the Union or out of the Union, or whether you simply consider it a connection or a disconnection with the other States; but to the extent that a State nullifies or sets aside any law or any provision of the Constitution, to that extent it has dissolved its connection, and no more. I think the States that have passed their personal liberty bills, in violation of the Constitution of the United States, coming in conflict with the fugitive slave law, to that extent have dissolved their connection, and to that extent it is revolution. But because some of the free States have passed laws violative of the Constitution; because they have, to some extent, dissolved their connection with this Government, does that justify us of the South in following that bad example? Because they have passed personal liberty bills, and have, to that extent, violated the compact which is reciprocal, shall we turn around, on the other hand, and violate the Constitution by coercing them to a compliance with it? Will we do so?

Then I come back to the starting point: let us stand in the Union and upon the Constitution; and if anybody is to leave this Union, or violate its guarantees, it shall be those who have taken the initiative, and passed their personal liberty bills. I am in the Union, and intend to stay in it. I intend to hold on to the Union, and the guarantees under which this Union has grown; and I do not intend to be driven from it, nor out of it, by their unconstitutional enactments.

Chapter 3

The Causes and Consequences of the Civil War

1

North-South Regional Differences Made the Conflict Inevitable

Charles A. Beard and Mary R. Beard

Prior to the Civil War, the Northern states—having already embraced the industrial revolution—viewed slavery, if not as a moral wrong, then as an institution whose time and usefulness was quickly passing. The Southern states—desperately trying to retain their agrarian-based society—viewed slavery as their "peculiar institution" and a central component to maintaining their way of life. In fact, they viewed the ability not only to maintain slavery but also to *expand* it into the territories as essential to ensuring economic stability in the South. A husband-and-wife historian team, Charles A. Beard and Mary R. Beard, provide a classic analysis of the differences between Northern and Southern cultures. Since Southern planting methods were rapidly depleting the soil, the South demanded the ability to expand into the territories in order to take advantage of rich, virgin land. Southern spokespersons also viewed the Northern fixation on the issue of slavery as simply a cover for "an underlying conspiracy against agriculture." In contrast, the cities of the Northeast and, increasingly, the Northwest were emerging as major industrial centers. Increased industrialization called for a proliferation of railroads and telegraph lines. A new way of life was emerging based upon free labor instead of slave labor. A clash between these different ways of life and economic forces seemed inevitable. The only question that remained was *when* the ultimate confrontation would occur.

Charles A. Beard and Mary R. Beard, "The Approach of the Irrepressible Conflict," *The Rise of American Civilization*, vol. 2. New York: Macmillan, 1927.

Had the economic systems of the North and the South remained static or changed slowly without effecting immense dislocations in the social structure, the balance of power might have been maintained indefinitely. . . . But nothing was stable in the economy of the United States or in the moral sentiments associated with its diversities.

Within each section of the country, the necessities of the productive system were generating portentous results. The periphery of the industrial vortex of the Northeast was daily enlarging, agriculture in the Northwest was being steadily supplemented by manufacturing, and the area of virgin soil open to exploitation by planters was diminishing with rhythmic regularity—shifting with mechanical precision the weights which statesmen had to adjust in their efforts to maintain the equilibrium of peace. Within each of the three sections also occurred an increasing intensity of social concentration as railways, the telegraph, and the press made travel and communication cheap and almost instantaneous, facilitating the centripetal process that was drawing people of similar economic status and parallel opinions into coöperative activities. Finally the intellectual energies released by accumulating wealth and growing leisure—stimulated by the expansion of the reading public and the literary market—developed with deepened accuracy the word-patterns of the current social persuasions, contributing with galvanic effect to the consolidation of identical groupings.

Industrial Interests versus Agricultural Interests

As the years passed, the planting leaders of Jefferson's agricultural party insisted with mounting fervor that the opposition, first of the Whigs and then of the Republicans, was at bottom an association of interests formed for the purpose of plundering productive management and labor on the land. And with steadfast insistence they declared that in the insatiable greed of their political foes lay the source of the dissensions which were tearing the country asunder.

"There is not a pursuit in which man is engaged (agriculture excepted)," exclaimed Reuben Davis of Mississippi in 1860, "which is not demanding legislative aid to enable it to enlarge its profits and all at the expense of the primary pursuit of man—agriculture. . . . Those interests, having a common purpose of plunder, have united and combined to use the government as the instrument of their operation and have thus virtually converted it into a consolidated empire. Now this combined host of interests stands arrayed against the agricultural states; and this is the reason of the conflict which like an earthquake is shaking our political fabric to its foundation." The furor over slavery is a mere subterfuge to cover other purposes. "Relentless avarice stands firm with its iron heel upon the Constitution." This creature, "incorporated avarice," has chained "the agricultural states to the northern rock" and lives like a vulture upon their prosperity. It is the effort of Prometheus to burst his manacles that provokes the assault on slavery. "These states struggle like a giant," continued Davis, "and alarm these incorporated interests, lest they may break the chain that binds them to usurpation; and therefore they are making this fierce onslaught upon the slave property of the southern states."

The area of virgin soil open to exploitation by planters was diminishing with rhythmic regularity.

The fact that free-soil advocates waged war only on slavery in the territories was to Jefferson Davis [of Mississippi] conclusive proof of an underlying conspiracy against agriculture. He professed more respect for the abolitionist than for the free-soiler. The former, he said, is dominated by an honest conviction that slavery is wrong everywhere and that all men ought to be free; the latter does not assail slavery in the states—he merely wishes to abolish it in the territories that are in due course to be admitted to the Union.

With challenging directness, Davis turned upon his opponents in the Senate and charged them with using slavery as a blind to delude the unwary: "What do you propose, gentlemen of the Free-Soil party? Do you propose to better the condition of the slave? Not at all. What then do you propose? You say you are opposed to the expansion of slavery. . . . Is the slave to be benefited by it? Not at all. It is not humanity that influences you in the position which you now occupy before the country. . . . It is that you may have an opportunity of cheating us that you want to limit slave territory within circumscribed bounds. It is that you may have a majority in the Congress of the United States and convert the Government into an engine of northern aggrandizement. It is that your section may grow in power and prosperity upon treasures unjustly taken from the South, like the vampire bloated and gorged with the blood which it has secretly sucked from its victim . . . You desire to weaken the political power of the southern states; and why? Because you want, by an unjust system of legislation, to promote the industry of the New England states, at the expense of the people of the South and their industry."

The furor over slavery is a mere subterfuge to cover other purposes.

Such in the mind of Jefferson Davis, fated to be president of the Confederacy, was the real purpose of the party which sought to prohibit slavery in the territories; that party did not declare slavery to be a moral disease calling for the severe remedy of the surgeon; it merely sought to keep bondage out of the new states as they came into the Union—with one fundamental aim in view, namely, to gain political ascendancy in the government of the United States and fasten upon the country an economic policy that meant the exploitation of the South for the benefit of northern capitalism.

But the planters were after all fighting against the census returns, as the phrase of the day ran current. The amazing growth of northern industries, the rapid extension of railways, the swift expansion of foreign trade to the ends of the earth, the attachment of the farming regions of the West to the centers of manufacture and finance through transportation and credit, the destruction of state consciousness by migration, the alien invasion, the erection of new commonwealths in the Valley of Democracy, the nationalistic drive of interstate commerce, the increase of population in the North, and the southward pressure of the capitalistic glacier all conspired to assure the ultimate triumph of what the orators were fond of calling "the free labor system." This was a dynamic thrust far too powerful for planters operating in a limited territory with incompetent labor on soil of diminishing fertility. Those who swept forward with it, exulting in the approaching triumph of machine industry, warned the planters of their ultimate subjection.

The Slavocracy

To statesmen of the invincible forces recorded in the census returns, the planting opposition was a huge, compact, and self-conscious economic association bent upon political objects—the possession of the government of the United States, the protection of its interests against adverse legislation, dominion over the territories, and enforcement of the national fugitive slave law throughout the length and breadth of the land. No phrase was more often on the lips of northern statesmen than "the slave power." The pages of the Congressional Globe bristled with references to "the slave system" and its influence over the government of the country. But it was left for [Senator] William H. Seward of New York to describe it with a fullness of familiar knowledge that made his characterization a classic.

No phrase was more often on the lips of northern statesmen than "the slave power."

Seward knew from experience that a political party was no mere platonic society engaged in discussing abstractions. "A party," he said, "is in one sense a joint stock association, in which those who contribute most direct the action and management of the concern. The slaveholders contributing in an overwhelming proportion to the capital strength of the Democratic party, they necessarily dictate and prescribe its policy. The inevitable caucus system enables them to do this with a show of fairness and justice." This class of slaveholders, consisting of only three hundred and forty-seven thousand persons, Seward went on to say, was spread from the banks of the Delaware to the banks of the Rio Grande; it possessed nearly all the real estate in that section, owned more than three million other "persons" who were denied all civil and political rights, and inhibited "freedom of speech, freedom of press, freedom of the ballot box, freedom of education, freedom of literature, and freedom of popular assemblies. . . . The slaveholding class has become the governing power in each of the slaveholding states and it practically chooses thirty of the sixty-two members of the Senate, ninety of the two hundred and thirty-three members of the House of Representatives, and one hundred and five of the two hundred and ninety-five electors of the President and Vice-President of the United States."

Becoming still more concrete, Seward accused the President [James Buchanan] of being "a confessed apologist of the slave-property class." Examining the composition of the Senate, he found the slave-owning group in possession of all the important committees. Peering into the House of Representatives he discovered no impregnable bulwark of freedom there. Nor did respect for judicial ermine compel him to spare the Supreme Court. With irony he exclaimed: "How fitting does the proclamation of its opening close with the invocation: 'God save the United States and this honorable court.'. . . The court consists of a chief justice and eight associate justices. Of these five were called from slave states and four from free states. The opinions and bias of each of them were carefully considered by the President and Senate when he was appointed. Not one of them was found wanting in soundness of politics, according to the slaveholder's exposition of the Constitution, and those who were called from the free states were even more distinguished in that respect than their brethren from the slaveholding states."

"It is an irrepressible conflict."

Seward then analyzed the civil service of the national government and could descry not a single person among the thousands employed in the post office, the treasury, and other great departments who was "false to the slaveholding interest." Under the spoils system, the dominion of the slavocracy extended into all branches of the federal administration. "The customs-houses and the public lands pour forth two golden streams—one into the elections to procure votes for the slaveholding class; and the other into the treasury to be enjoyed by those whom it shall see fit to reward with places in the public service." Even in the North, religion, learning, and the press were under the spell of this masterful class, frightened lest they incur its wrath.

Having described the gigantic operating structure of the slavocracy, Seward drew with equal power a picture of the opposing system founded on "free labor." He surveyed the course of economy in the North—the growth of industry, the spread of railways, the swelling tide of European immigration, and the westward roll of free farmers—rounding out the country, knitting it together, bringing "these antagonistic systems" continually into closer contact. Then he uttered those fateful words which startled conservative citizens from Maine to California—words of prophecy which proved to be brutally true—"the irrepressible conflict."

The Irrepressible Conflict

This inexorable clash, he said, was not "accidental, unnecessary, the work of interested or fanatical agitators and therefore ephemeral." No. "It is an irrepressible conflict between opposing and enduring forces." The hopes of those who sought peace by appealing to slave owners to reform themselves were as chaff in a storm. "How long and with what success have you waited already for that reformation? Did any property class ever so reform itself? Did the patricians in old Rome, the noblesse or clergy in France? The landholders in Ireland? The landed aristocracy in England? Does the slaveholding class even seek to beguile you with such a hope? Has it not become rapacious, arrogant, defiant?" All attempts at compromise were "vain and ephemeral." There was accordingly but one supreme task before the people of the United States—the task of confounding and overthrowing "by one decisive blow the betrayers of the Constitution and freedom forever.". . .

Given an irrepressible conflict which could be symbolized in such unmistakable patterns by competent interpreters of opposing factions, a transfer of the issues from the forum to the field, from the conciliation of diplomacy to the decision of arms was bound to come. Each side obdurately bent upon its designs and convinced of its rectitude, by the fulfillment of its wishes precipitated events and effected distributions of power that culminated finally in the tragedy foretold by Seward.

2

The Civil War Was a War of Aggression by the North Against the South

James Ronald Kennedy and Walter Donald Kennedy

During the crisis years preceding the Civil War, a rallying cry for those Southerners who favored secession was that of "states' rights." That term referred to the power of each individual state to determine the laws and rights of the citizens within its own borders. The concept of states' rights also came to symbolize the Southern states' struggle with the federal government over the issue of slavery. In the excerpts that follow, James Ronald Kennedy and Walter Donald Kennedy, brothers who are descendants of a Civil War soldier, emphatically argue that the right of states to act as sovereign entities was established by the Constitution. They also assert that from the inception of the U.S. government, the "sovereign authority of the states" was clearly reserved. Finally, they determine that when the Southern states seceded, they exercised their last major act as sovereign entities.

O ne of the many arguments used against the Jeffersonian school of limited central government, and later against secession, was that the states were never sovereign. The Yankee president Abraham Lincoln even went so far as to claim that the Union preceded the states. . . . An explanation of what is meant by the term "sovereignty" may be useful at this point. The state government is not sovereign, nor is any citizen individually. By the term "sovereign state" we refer to the citizens of the state collectively. John C. Calhoun described the state as the "sovereign community." The state, as the agent of the people, exercises sovereign authority by the consent of those who created it (i.e., the people of the state). A state, as the agent of the sovereign community, may delegate a portion of its power to another government, but it can not delegate a portion of sovereignty. Sovereignty, like chastity, is not transferable or divisible.

The states did not renounce their sovereign authority by ratifying the Constitution.

Prior to the signing of the Declaration of Independence, the colonies had within their control the right of colonial legislation. Many of the colonies had removed their royal appointed governors, and Virginia had gone so far as to declare her independence in May of 1776! All these events were the acts of a sovereign nature, with no reference to a higher governmental authority. When, on July 4, 1776, they declared their independence it was a joint declaration announcing to the world that the thirteen American colonies were now free and independent states (note the plural), not in the aggregate as one nation but individually, yet acting jointly as may best secure for all the blessings of liberty. So from their separate and independent acts prior to and at the time of their declaration of independence, these colonies, now states, acted separately and independently of each other without reference to a superior governmental agency and in their capacity as sovereign entities.

During the Revolutionary War they continued as sovereign states. . . .

At the close of the Revolutionary War, did His Britannic Majesty recognize the independence of the United States alone according to the *e pluribus unum* model (i.e., as one nation)? No! Each state is named as a free and independent state in the Treaty of Paris signed by the representatives of the British Monarch.

Additional evidence demonstrating sovereign nature of the individual American states can be found in the language of the Articles of Confederation. In Article II the states make known to all parties that:

> Each State retains its sovereignty, freedom, and inde-
> pendence, and every power, jurisdiction, and right,
> which is not by this Confederation expressly delegated
> to the United States in Congress assembled.

Language can not be clearer. There is no room to question the states' intent to maintain their individual "sovereignty." The states acceded to the Articles of Confederation as sovereign entities and reserved all powers unto themselves as separate and independent states. It is also instructive to observe the relationship between these sovereign states in Congress under the Articles of Confederation. Each state voted as a unit, with an equal vote regardless of the size of its population or territory. Why did the states treat each other as equals? The answer is simple if we understand the principle of state sovereignty. How else could sovereign states treat each other absent a treaty, compact, or constitution mutually agreed to that plainly altered international convention? In international relations, when a league between sovereign nations is established, each nation is presumed equal unless the presumption has been specifically altered and agreed to by all parties to the league. . . .

The states exercised their sovereign authority prior to their joint declaration of independence, during the American War for Independence, their sovereignty was recognized by the British Monarch by acknowledging their independence, and the states maintained their sovereign status under the terms of the Articles of Confederation. Now arises the question: Did these sovereign states surrender or renounce state sovereignty by the ratification of the United States Constitution?

The Sovereign Authority of the States

The Constitution clearly established a different government from the one which operated under the Articles of Confederation. The preamble to the Constitution boldly states that "We the People of the United States . . ." The monarchists, Federalists, consolidationists, and others favoring a strong central federal government have seized upon these words as evidence that the people of America formed a national government, superior to the states. If this assertion is correct, then it follows that sovereign authority has shifted from the states to the central government. Did the people of America hold a plebiscite and, by virtue of the democratic principle of majority rule, vote to establish the federal government as the national and supreme government of the United States? The answer, as any school child should know, is a simple no. The Constitution was proposed by representatives of the individual states and ratified by the states, becoming binding only on those states which so ratified it. In other words, the people of the United States as a collective body did not participate in the process, the states participated in their independent and sovereign role as the elected agent of the people of their respective states. In their acts of ratification, many states specifically reserved the right to recall their delegated sovereign powers should those powers be used by the federal government to encroach upon the rights and liberties of the people. This reservation of rights is another example of the states exercising their sovereign authority. From these examples we can see that the states did not renounce their sovereign authority by ratifying the Constitution.

We have now observed that the states, acting in their separate and independent capacity, exercised their sovereign authority; prior to their Fourth of July joint declaration of independence, during the Revolutionary War, their separate independence was recognized by the British Crown; they restated their separate and independent nature in the Articles of Confederation and, as separate and independent states, sent representatives to the Constitutional Convention; and subsequently, as sovereign states, they ratified the new Constitution contingent upon certain reservations of rights. Throughout this entire course of events, state sovereignty was in no way reduced, impaired, encumbered, or otherwise compromised. Sovereignty remained where it was originally—with the states and the people thereof. The question now arises: Did the states, by some specific declaration in the newly ratified Constitution, surrender their sovereignty to the central federal government?

The Constitution and State Sovereignty

International law requires more than an inference or even a series of inferences to determine that a nation has voluntarily surrendered its sovereignty in favor of another government. The same rule holds for the thirteen sovereign states that joined together under the compact of the Constitution to form the federal government. The states, by their own voluntary action, created as their common agent the federal government. By means of a compact the states delegated specific powers to their common agent. Their agent, the federal government, could act only in those specific areas allowed by the Constitution. Notice that nowhere in the Constitution is sovereignty specifically surrendered or transferred to the federal government. Even though this new compact limited the federal government to specific areas, there were numerous demands for an amendment similar to Article II in the Articles of Confederation to ensure that the sovereignty of the states would remain safe from the centralizing (monarchial) tendency of all governments. Thus the Ninth and Tenth Amendments were immediately added to the Constitution. The Tenth Amendment clearly states that all powers not delegated by the Constitution are reserved to the states. At the inception of the United States Constitutional Convention, the sovereign authority of the states, as we have demonstrated, was held to remain with the states. Article V of the Constitution provides that no state shall be denied equal suffrage in the Senate without its consent. This article recognizes the sovereign authority of the state to defend its equal representation in the Senate. Article IV, Section 3.1, provides that no state may be formed within the territory of an existing state without its consent. Who may nullify the will of Congress, the president, the Supreme Court, all other states, and the people of the United States in the aggregate, if they decide to form a new state within an existing state, contrary to the will of that existing state? By its provisions in Article IV, Section 3.1, the Constitution allows the threatened state to nullify the actions of the federal government, combinations of states, and/or the numerical majority of citizens. Article I transfers the war-making power from the sovereign states to the federal government, but the sovereign states retain the right to engage in war if in imminent danger. Such is the nature of a sovereign state—it possesses the right of self-defense!

Attacks Against State Sovereignty

As we have seen, the monarchists were defeated in their early attempts to establish a strong central government patterned after the British system. They gradually moved into the Federalist camp and continued to work for a consolidation of power in the federal government. It is difficult today to assess the motives of the Federalists. Some, such as John Adams and Alexander Hamilton, were monarchists. Others, like George Washington perhaps, recalled the difficulty of defending the country when faced with an organized foreign power and feared future foreign invasion if European powers perceived the United States as a weak and disorganized country. Some, like James Madison, honestly believed that the states were a greater threat to the federal government and therefore the central government needed more powers to protect itself from state encroachments upon federal powers. Surely there were many who had honest motives for desiring a stronger (as opposed to an all-powerful) federal government. In the final analysis, the primary motivating factor encouraging the consolidation of power was one of commercial greed—in a word, "money." Patrick Henry made it very clear that the purpose of the Revolutionary War was to secure for Americans not a "great and mighty empire" but the blessings of "liberty" (often described as the right to be left alone). This view was not shared by the writers of the *Federalist Papers* who declared it to be their intention to establish an American commercial empire. The Northeastern states desired to close the Mississippi River by giving control of it to Spain, thereby forcing trade eastward. They were also fearful that an expanding West (a substantial portion of which was then owned by Virginia) would draw off their labor supply and thus increase their cost of labor. In short, the Northeastern mercantile interest feared a loss of their political and economic control of an expanding, agricultural America. Gouverneur Morris of Massachusetts wanted to give control of the Mississippi River to Spain because he thought this would allow the Eastern states to hold the population of the West under their control. Captain James De Wolf, one of Rhode Island's most prosperous slaver traders, realized the potential in developing manufacturing in the United States. He transferred capital from his slaving enterprises and built one of the earliest cotton mills in the New England states. . . . Slowly political philosophy of limited versus centralized government began to take on a commercial character as the Northern states began to turn to the federal government as a source of money for internal improvements and of protection for its emerging commercial empire. The money for internal improvements in the North was derived to a greater extent from the Southern states. In the words of Virginia's senator William Grayson, the South had become the "milch cow of the Union"!

With the ratification of the Constitution, the two opposing political theories stood face to face waiting to see who would draw first blood.

With the ratification of the Constitution, the two opposing political theories stood face to face waiting to see who would draw first blood. It did not take long. One of the very first attempts of the Federalists to enlarge the power of the federal government, to the detriment of the states, was made by none other than the United States Supreme Court in *Chisholm v. Georgia*. A basic principle of sovereignty is that the sovereign power can not be brought under the jurisdiction of a court. In this case, an individual had brought suit in federal court against the sovereign state of Georgia. The states were shocked! They had been assured by no less a personage than Hamilton himself that this immunity from suit was "inherent in the nature of sovereignty." John Marshall, who would later work so hard to enlarge the power of the federal government, had declared thusly:

> I hope that no gentleman will think that a State will be called at the bar of the Federal court. . . . It is not rational to suppose that the sovereign power should be dragged before a court.

The state of Georgia declared that to submit to the jurisdiction of the federal court would be to destroy the "retained sovereignty of the State." The Federalist United States Supreme Court required only fourteen days to hear and decide the case and issue a four to one decision commanding Georgia to submit to the authority of the federal court. The Georgia legislature passed a bill ordering that any federal agent attempting to execute the court's order should ". . . suffer death, without benefit of clergy, by being hanged." Eleven of the thirteen states immediately ratified the Eleventh Amendment declaring that the United States Supreme Court has no judicial power to hear a suit against a state brought by an individual. The Supreme Court had acted so unconstitutionally in the Chisholm case that it required an immediate constitutional amendment to protect state sovereignty. . . .

The struggle between the proponents of state sovereignty and those favoring centralized Federalism would continue until the numerical majority of the North at last seized complete control of the federal government. When the Southern states seceded, the North saw its "milch cow" escaping and waged aggressive war against the South to maintain its commercial empire. The South was at last conquered and turned into a colonial province of the Yankee empire. What most Americans do not understand is that state sovereignty is the primary principle upon which the Constitutional Federal Republic was established. Our liberties and freedoms as Americans can not be guaranteed and protected without state sovereignty. Recall federal Judge Chase's words, "State Sovereignty died at Appomattox." He was right, state sovereignty died with the Confederate States of America—slain by the commercial and political interest of the Northern numerical majority.

3

The Civil War Ensured America's Development as an Industrial Capitalist Nation

James M. McPherson

At the war's end in 1865, the consequences of the South's defeat went beyond the loss of human life. To be sure, the over 620,000 combined dead on both sides of the battlefield was a horrific tally never to be matched again, to this day, in U.S. history. However, as James M. McPherson explains in the following selection, in addition to the lives lost, the war signaled a new start for the country. The balance of political power shifted from the South to the North. Industrial capitalism would shape the future of the nation and the world. More than that, after the war the country was increasingly perceived as one nation, not a union of states: This distinction marked the beginning of a new vision and a new social reality within America. James M. McPherson is the George Henry Davis '86 Professor of American History at Princeton University. He won the Pulitzer Prize in history in 1989 for his book *Battle Cry of Freedom: The Civil War Era*, from which this selection was excerpted.

Arguments about the causes and consequences of the Civil War, as well as the reasons for northern victory, will continue as long as there are historians to wield the

James M. McPherson, *Battle Cry of Freedom: The Civil War Era*. New York: Oxford University Press, Inc., 1998. Copyright © 1998 by Oxford University Press, Inc. Reproduced by permission.

121

pen—which is, perhaps even for this bloody conflict, mightier than the sword. But certain large consequences of the war seem clear. Secession and slavery were killed, never to be revived during the century and a quarter since Appomattox. These results signified a broader transformation of American society and polity punctuated if not alone achieved by the war. Before 1861 the two words "United States" were generally rendered as a plural noun: "the United States *are* a republic." The war marked a transition of the United States to a singular noun. The "Union" also became the nation, and Americans now rarely speak of their Union except in an historical sense. Lincoln's wartime speeches betokened this transition. In his first inaugural address he used the word "Union" twenty times and the word "nation" not once. In his first message to Congress, on July 4, 1861, he used "Union" thirty-two times and "nation" three times. In his letter to Horace Greeley of August 22, 1862, on the relationship of slavery to the war, Lincoln spoke of the Union eight times and of the nation not at all. Little more than a year later, in his address at Gettysburg, the president did not refer to the "Union" at all but used the word "nation" five times to invoke a new birth of freedom and nationalism for the United States. And in his second inaugural address, looking back over the events of the past four years, Lincoln spoke of one side seeking to dissolve the *Union* in 1861 and the other accepting the challenge of war to preserve the *nation.*

This change in the federal balance paralleled a radical shift of political power from South to North.

The old federal republic in which the national government had rarely touched the average citizen except through the post-office gave way to a more centralized polity that taxed the people directly and created an internal revenue bureau to collect these taxes, drafted men into the army, expanded the jurisdiction of federal courts, created a national currency and a national banking system, and established the first national agency for social welfare—the Freedmen's Bureau. Eleven of the first twelve amendments to the Constitution had limited the powers of the national government;

six of the next seven, beginning with the Thirteenth Amendment in 1865, vastly expanded those powers at the expense of the states.

A Shift in Power

This change in the federal balance paralleled a radical shift of political power from South to North. During the first seventy-two years of the republic down to 1861 a slaveholding resident of one of the states that joined the Confederacy had been President of the United States for forty-nine of those years—more than two-thirds of the time. In Congress, twenty-three of the thirty-six speakers of the House and twenty-four of the presidents pro tem of the Senate had been southerners. The Supreme Court always had a southern majority; twenty of the thirty-five justices to 1861 had been appointed from slave states. After the war a century passed before a resident of an ex-Confederate state was elected president. For half a century *none* of the speakers of the House or presidents pro tem of the Senate came from the South, and only five of the twenty-six Supreme Court justices appointed during that half-century were southerners.

These figures symbolize a sharp and permanent change

Freed slaves gather in Charleston at the end of the Civil War. The war's end marked the beginning of the shift toward a free-labor economy in America.

in the direction of American development. Through most of American history the South has seemed different from the rest of the United States, with [as stated by Monroe L. Billington] "a separate and unique identity . . . which appeared to be out of the mainstream of American experience." But when did the northern stream become the mainstream? From a broader perspective it may have been the *North* that was exceptional and unique before the Civil War. The South more closely resembled a majority of the societies in the world than did the rapidly changing North during the antebellum generation. Despite the abolition of legal slavery or serfdom throughout much of the western hemisphere and western Europe, most of the world—like the South—had an unfree or quasi-free labor force. Most societies in the world remained predominantly rural, agricultural, and labor-intensive; most, including even several European countries, had illiteracy rates as high or higher than the South's 45 percent; most like the South remained bound by traditional values and networks of family, kinship, hierarchy, and patriarchy. The North—along with a few countries of northwestern Europe—hurtled forward eagerly toward a future of industrial capitalism that many southerners found distasteful if not frightening; the South remained proudly and even defiantly rooted in the past before 1861.

Union victory in the war destroyed the southern vision of America and ensured that the northern vision would become the American vision.

Thus when secessionists protested that they were acting to preserve traditional rights and values, they were correct. They fought to protect their constitutional liberties against the perceived northern threat to overthrow them. The South's concept of republicanism had not changed in three-quarters of a century; the North's had. With complete sincerity the South fought to preserve its version of the republic of the founding fathers—a government of limited powers that protected the rights of property and whose constituency comprised an independent gentry and yeomanry of the white race undisturbed by large cities, heartless factories, restless free workers, and class conflict. The accession to power of the Republican party, with its ideology of competitive, egalitarian, free-labor capitalism, was a signal to the South that the northern majority had turned irrevocably toward this frightening, revolutionary future. Indeed, the Black Republican party appeared to the eyes of many southerners as "essentially a revolutionary party" composed of "a motley throng of Sans culottes . . . Infidels and freelovers, interspersed by Bloomer women, fugitive slaves, and amalgamationists" [as stated by the *New Orleans Daily Delta* and Steven A. Channing]. Therefore secession was a pre-emptive counterrevolution to prevent the Black Republican revolution from engulfing the South. "*We* are not revolutionists," insisted James B.D. DeBow and Jefferson Davis during the Civil War, "We are resisting revolution. . . . We are conservative."

Union victory in the war destroyed the southern vision of America and ensured that the northern vision would become the American vision. Until 1861, however, it was the North that was out of the mainstream, not the South. Of course the northern states, along with Britain and a few countries in northwestern Europe, were cutting a new channel in world history that would doubtless have become the mainstream even if the American Civil War had not happened. Russia had abolished serfdom in 1861 to complete the dissolution of this ancient institution of bound labor in Europe. But for Americans the Civil War marked the turning point. A Louisiana planter who returned home sadly after the war wrote in 1865: "Society has been completely changed by the war. The [French] revolution of '89 did not produce a greater change in the 'Ancien Régime' than this has in our social life." And four years later George Ticknor, a retired Harvard professor, concluded that the Civil War had created a "great gulf between what happened before in our century and what has happened since, or what is likely to happen hereafter. It does not seem to me as if I were living in the country in which I was born." From the war sprang the great flood that caused the stream of American history to surge into a new channel and transferred the burden of exceptionalism from North to South.

4

The Civil War Caused Dramatic Changes in Black-White Relations

C. Vann Woodward

During the time of slavery, there was an enforced closeness between blacks and whites in the South as well as a system of mutual obligations that resulted from the maintenance of plantation life and the master/slave relationship. One of the major consequences of the Civil War—the end of slavery—introduced the necessity for a marked change in the entire system of relationships between blacks and whites. Historian C. Vann Woodward, one of the foremost experts on the history and evolution of race relations in the United States, examines the relations between blacks and whites immediately after the Civil War yet before the institution of Jim Crow (legalized racial segregation). He concludes that while elements of the slavery regime were still in place, and some forms of enforced segregation began immediately, an exceptional degree of egalitarianism existed between the races.

In the South the traumatic experiences of Civil War, invasion, defeat, emancipation, occupation, and reconstruction had profound and complex—sometimes contradictory—effects on racial relations. The immediate response to the collapse of slavery was often a simultaneous withdrawal of both races from the enforced intimacy and the more burdensome obligations imposed by the old regime on each. Denied the benefits of slavery, whites shook off its responsibilities—excess hands, dependents too old or too ill or too young to work, tenants too poor to pay rent. Freedmen for their part often fled old masters and put behind them old grievances, hatreds, and the scene of old humiliations. One of the most momentous of racial separations was the voluntary withdrawal of the Negroes from the white-dominated Protestant churches, often over white protest, in order to establish and control their own separate religious institutions. In these and other ways the new order added physical distance to social distance between the races.

Segregation Immediately After the War

The separations were not all voluntary. Whites clung unwaveringly to the old doctrine of white supremacy and innate Negro inferiority that had been sustained by the old regime. It still remained to be seen what institutions or laws or customs would be necessary to maintain white control now that slavery was gone. Under slavery, control was best maintained by a large degree of physical contact and association. Under the strange new order the old methods were not always available or applicable, though the contacts and associations they produced did not all disappear at once. To the dominant whites it began to appear that the new order required a certain amount of compulsory separation of the races.

Race relations . . . could not be said to have crystalized or stabilized.

The temporary anarchy that followed the collapse of the old discipline produced a state of mind bordering on hysteria among Southern white people. The first year a great fear of black insurrection and revenge seized many minds, and for a longer time the conviction prevailed that Negroes could not be induced to work without compulsion. Large numbers of temporarily uprooted freedmen roamed the highways, congested in towns and cities, or joined the federal militia. In the presence of these conditions the provisional legislatures established by President [Andrew] Johnson in 1865 adopted the notorious Black Codes. Some of them were intended to establish systems of peonage [where servants work until debts are paid] or apprenticeship resembling slavery. . . .

Other aspects of segregation appeared early and widely and were sanctioned by Reconstruction authorities. The most conspicuous of these was the segregation of the public schools. While the law might not provide for it and individuals might deplore it, segregation of the schools nevertheless took place promptly and prevailed continuously. There were very few exceptions. . . . The law sometimes provided for separate facilities for the races during Reconstruction. But even when this was not the case, and when both races were housed in the same jails, hospitals, or asylums, they were usually quartered in separate cells, floors, or wings. All these practices, legal or extra-legal, had the consent or at least the acquiescence of the Reconstruction governments.

For a time old and new rubbed shoulders . . . in a manner that differed significantly from Jim Crow of the future or slavery of the past.

In view of the degree of racial separation developed during Reconstruction, some historians have concluded that the full-blown Jim Crow system sprang up immediately after the end of slavery to take the place of the Peculiar Institution. In a full and interesting study of the Negro in South Carolina entitled *After Slavery*, Joel Williamson finds that while 'slavery necessitated a constant, physical intimacy,' emancipation precipitated an immediate and revolutionary separation of races. 'Well before the end of Reconstruction,' he writes, 'separation had crystalized into a comprehensive pattern which, in its essence, remained unaltered until the middle of the twentieth century.'

Between Slavery and Jim Crow: An Unfamiliar Racial Order

The experience of South Carolina may have been exceptional in some respects. But in most parts of the South, including South Carolina, race relations during Reconstruction could not be said to have crystalized or stabilized nor to have become what they later became. There were too many cross currents and contradictions, revolutionary innovations and violent reactions. Racial relations of the old-regime pattern often persisted stubbornly into the new order and met head-on with interracial encounters of an entirely new and sometimes equalitarian type. Freedman and white man might turn from a back-door encounter of the traditional sort to a strained man-to-man contact of the awkward new type within the same day. Black faces continued to appear at the back door, but they also began to appear in wholly unprecedented and unexpected places—in the jury box and on the judge's bench, in council chamber and legislative hall, at the polls and the market place. Neither of these contrasting types of contact, the old or the new, was stable or destined to endure for very long, but for a time old and new rubbed shoulders—and so did black and white—in a manner that differed significantly from Jim Crow [legalized segregation]

Following the Civil War, many whites were alarmed to see blacks exercising newly acquired freedoms such as voting.

of the future or slavery of the past.

What happened in North Carolina was a revelation to conservative whites. 'It is amazing,' wrote Kemp Battle of Raleigh, 'how quietly our people take negro juries, or rather negroes on juries.' Randolph Shotwell of Ruther-fordton was dismayed on seeing 'long processions of countrymen entering the village by the various roads mounted and afoot, whites and blacks marching together, and in frequent instances arm-in-arm, a sight to disgust even a decent negro.' It was disturbing even to native white radicals, as one of them admitted in the Raleigh *Standard*, to find at times 'the two races now eat together at the same table, sit together in the same room, work together, visit and hold debating societies together.' It is not that such occurrences were typical or very common, but that they could happen at all that was important.

Blacks Freely Exercise Freedom

Southern Negroes responded to news of the Reconstruction Act of March 1867 [passed by Congress in reaction to Southern States' persecution of blacks] with numerous demonstrations against incipient Jim Crowism. In New Orleans they demonstrated so vigorously and persistently against the Jim Crow 'Star Cars' [separate street cars for blacks] established in 1864 that General Phil Sheridan ordered an end to racial discrimination on street cars in May 1867. Similar demonstrations and what would now be called 'sit-ins' brought an end about the same time to segregated street cars in Richmond, Charleston, and other cities. One of the strongest demands of the freedmen upon the new radical state legislatures of 1868 in South Carolina and Mississippi was for civil rights laws that would protect their rights on common carriers and public accommodations. The law makers of those states and others responded with comprehensive anti-discrimination statutes. Their impact was noted in South Carolina in 1868 by Elizabeth H. Botume, a Northern teacher, on a previously segregated river steamer from Charleston to Beaufort. She witnessed 'a decided change' among Negro passengers, previously excluded from the upper deck. 'They were everywhere,' she wrote, 'choosing the best staterooms and best seats at the table. Two prominent colored members of the State Legislature were on board with their families. There were also several well-known Southerners, still uncompromising rebels. It was a curious scene and full of significance.' In North Carolina shortly after the adoption of the Federal Civil Rights Act of 1875 Negroes in various parts of the state successfully tested their rights in railroads, steamboats, hotels, theaters, and other public accommodations. One Negro took the railroad from Raleigh to Savannah and reported no difficulty riding and dining unsegregated. Future Congressman James E. O'Hara, a Negro, successfully integrated a steamer from Greenville to Tarboro.

It would be a mistaken effort to equate this period in racial relations with either the old regime of slavery or with the future rule of Jim Crow.

As a rule, however, Negroes were not aggressive in pressing their rights, even after they were assured them by law and protected in exercising them by the federal presence. It was easier to avoid painful rebuff or insult by refraining from the test of rights. Negroes rarely intruded upon hotels or restaurants where they were unwelcome. Whites often withdrew from desegregated facilities or cut down their patronage. Negro spokesmen constantly reiterated their disavowal of aspirations for what they called 'social equality' and insisted that they were concerned only for 'public equality,' by which they apparently meant civil and political rights. Actually there is little evidence of racial mixing on social occasions during Reconstruction, though there was much mixing on public occasions, particularly of a political character. Native white Republicans were conscious of their minority status and their desperate need for black support. As one of them wrote the Governor of Alabama, 'we must have men who will mix with the negroes & tell them of their rights. If we don't have such men, we will be defeated.' Such men, native white Alabamians, were found and they worked with a will across the color line.

End to an Exceptional Time

It would be wrong to exaggerate the amount of interracial association and intimacy produced during Reconstruction or to misconstrue its character and meaning. If the intimacy of the old regime [of slavery] had its unhappy and painful aspects, so did that of the new order. Unlike the quality of mercy, it was strained. It was also temporary, and it was usually self-conscious. It was a product of contrived circumstances, and neither race had time to become fully accustomed to the change or feel natural in the relationship. Nevertheless, it would be a mistaken effort to equate this period in racial relations with either the old regime of slavery or with the future rule of Jim Crow. It was too exceptional. It is impossible to conceive of innumerable events and interracial experiments and contacts of the 1860's taking place in the 1900's. To attempt that would be to do violence to the nuances of history.

Chronology

1820

The Missouri Compromise passes Congress. In addition to jointly admitting Missouri as a slave state and Maine as a free state, the law forbids slavery in all Louisiana Purchase lands north of 36°30' (except Missouri).

1845–1848

The American annexation of Texas and victory in the Mexican War starts the debate on whether newly acquired territories should permit slavery. The Wilmot Proviso is proposed, calling for no slavery in any territory acquired in the Mexican War. The bill passes in the House of Representatives but not in the Senate.

1850

Senator Henry Clay launches the Senate debate on what will become the Compromise of 1850. The bill passes and is signed into law by President Millard Fillmore. Among the bill's provisions, the slave trade is abolished in Washington, D.C., and a new, more restrictive Fugitive Slave Law is enacted, with heavy penalties for those who interfere with the capture and return of escaped slaves. California is admitted to the Union as a free state; New Mexico and Utah are admitted as territories, with the power to decide on their own whether to permit slavery (a doctrine known as popular sovereignty).

1852

Uncle Tom's Cabin by Harriet Beecher Stowe is published. This book, which indicts slavery and Northern complicity in it, is a popular success in the North but causes much alarm in the South.

1854

The Kansas-Nebraska Act is passed in Congress, voiding the 1820 Missouri Compromise and potentially extending slavery into territories north of 36°30' under the doctrine of popular sovereignty. The act is published by Senator Stephen A.

Douglas of Illinois; it is supported by Southern senators and congressmen but is bitterly opposed by Northerners.

1855–1856

The Kansas territory becomes a political and military battleground over the issue of slavery's expansion. Both "slave" and "free" factions seek recognition from Washington.

1857

The Supreme Court decision of *Dred Scott v. Sandford* is announced. The Court rules that blacks are not citizens and therefore cannot bring suit in federal courts; that since slaves are property, they may be taken anywhere in the United States without losing their slave status; and that the Missouri Compromise establishing a border between slave and free territory was unconstitutional.

1858

Illinois senator Stephen Douglas and Republican nominee Abraham Lincoln engage in a series of debates on slavery and race relations as they vie for Douglas's Senate seat.

1859

John Brown launches an unsuccessful raid on Harpers Ferry, Virginia, in the hope of triggering a general slave revolt.

1860

Abraham Lincoln wins the Republican presidential nomination. The Republican platform opposes slavery in the territories and supports the admission of Kansas as a free state. Lincoln is elected president of the United States.

December 20, 1860

South Carolina becomes the first state to secede from the Union.

January 9, 1861

Mississippi secedes from the Union.

January 10–February 1, 1861

Florida, Alabama, Georgia, Louisiana, and Texas secede.

February–March 1861

Delegates from the seven seceded states meet in Montgomery, Alabama, to form the Confederate States of America. Jefferson Davis is inaugurated as the Confederate president.

March 4, 1861
Lincoln is inaugurated as the sixteenth president of the United States.

April 12–14, 1861
Confederate guns open fire on the Union's Fort Sumter in Charleston, South Carolina. The Confederate flag is raised over the fort.

April 19, 1861
Lincoln orders a naval blockade of Southern ports.

July 21, 1861
Confederate soldiers are victorious at the First Battle of Bull Run (Manassas).

February 1862
Union forces under General Ulysses S. Grant score important victories in Tennessee.

March 9, 1862
The world's first battle between two ironclad ships, the Union *Monitor* and the Confederate *Merrimac*, ends in a draw.

April 16, 1862
The Confederate Congress enacts the first conscription law in American history.

September 24, 1862
Lincoln suspends the writ of habeas corpus throughout the North and subjects "all persons discouraging voluntary enlistments" to martial law.

January 1, 1863
The Emancipation Proclamation takes effect. The proclamation in its final form lays more emphasis on the enlisting of black soldiers; by late spring, recruiting is under way throughout the North and Union-occupied areas in the South.

March 3, 1863
Congress enacts a draft to raise troops; the law makes most male citizens age twenty to forty-five liable for conscription.

May 1–4, 1863
In a brilliant display of military tactics, Confederate general Robert E. Lee defeats a larger Union force in the Battle of Chancellorsville.

June 3, 1863
Lee leads seventy-five thousand Confederate soldiers in a campaign that will take them to Pennsylvania and culminate in the Battle of Gettysburg.

July 1–3, 1863
During the Battle of Gettysburg, twenty-three thousand Confederate and twenty-eight thousand Union soldiers are killed, wounded, or missing; this Union victory marks the end of the last major Confederate offensive of the war.

July 4, 1863
The town of Vicksburg, Mississippi, surrenders to Grant, ending a six-week siege; the importance of this victory ranks with that of Gettysburg.

November 19, 1863
Lincoln delivers his Gettysburg Address.

March 12, 1864
Ulysses S. Grant is placed in command of all Union armies.

June 7, 1864
Lincoln is renominated for president by the Republican Party; Andrew Johnson, a Tennessee Democrat who remained loyal to the Union, is named his running mate.

November 8, 1864
Lincoln is reelected, carrying all but three states.

January 31, 1865
Congress approves the Thirteenth Amendment to the Constitution, which abolishes slavery.

April 9, 1865
Lee surrenders to Grant at Appomattox Courthouse.

April 14, 1865
Lincoln is assassinated by John Wilkes Booth, a Confederate sympathizer; Andrew Johnson assumes the presidency.

December 13, 1865
The Thirteenth Amendment to the Constitution is ratified by the states.

For Further Research

Books

Robert C. Baron, ed., *Soul of America: Documenting Our Past.* Vol. 2. Golden, CO: North American Press, 1994.

Roy P. Basler, ed., *Abraham Lincoln: His Speeches and Writings.* New York: World, 1946.

———, ed., *The Collected Works of Abraham Lincoln.* New Brunswick, NJ: Rutgers University Press, 1953.

Charles A. Beard and Mary R. Beard, *The Rise of American Civilization.* New York: Macmillan, 1927.

Lilian Marie Briggs, ed., *Noted Speeches of Daniel Webster, Henry Clay, John C. Calhoun.* New York: Moffat, Yard, 1912.

Marshall L. DeRosa, ed., *The Quest for a National Identity and the American Civil War: The Politics of Dissolution.* New Brunswick, NJ: Transaction Publishers, 1998.

Philip S. Foner, ed., *Frederick Douglass: Selections from His Writings.* New York: International Publishers, 1964.

William W. Freehling and Craig M. Simpson, eds., *Secession Debated: Georgia's Showdown in 1860.* New York: Oxford University Press, 1992.

William Lloyd Garrison, *Selections from the Writings and Speeches of William Lloyd Garrison.* New York: Negro Universities Press, 1968.

Holman Hamilton, *Prologue to Conflict: The Crisis and Compromise of 1850.* Lexington: University of Kentucky Press, 1964.

Robert W. Johannsen, *The Letters of Stephen A. Douglas.* Urbana: University of Illinois Press, 1961.

James Ronald Kennedy and Walter Donald Kennedy, *The South Was Right!* Gretna, LA: Pelican, 1994.

Eric L. McKitrick, ed., *Slavery Defended: The Views of the Old South.* Englewood Cliffs, NJ: Prentice-Hall, 1963.

James M. McPherson, *Battle Cry of Freedom: The Civil War Era*. New York: Oxford University Press, 1988.

Allan Nevins, *Ordeal of the Union*. Vol. 2. New York: Charles Scribner's Sons, 1947.

Howard Cecil Perkins, ed., *Northern Editorials on Secession*. Vol. 1. Gloucester, MA: American Historical Association, 1964.

Roger L. Ransom, *Conflict and Compromise: The Political Economy of Slavery, Emancipation, and the American Civil War*. New York: Cambridge University Press, 1989.

James Ford Rhodes, *History of the United States from the Compromise of 1850*. Ed. Allan Nevins. Chicago: University of Chicago Press, 1966.

Kenneth M. Stampp, ed., *The Causes of the Civil War*. New York: Simon & Schuster, 1991.

Hans L. Trefousse, ed., *The Causes of the Civil War: Institutional Failure or Human Blunder?* New York: Holt, Rinehart, and Winston, 1971.

Jon L. Wakelyn, ed., *Southern Pamphlets on Secession: November 1860–April 1861*. Chapel Hill: University of North Carolina Press, 1996.

C. Vann Woodward, *The Strange Career of Jim Crow*. New York: Oxford University Press, 1974.

David Zarefsky, *Lincoln, Douglas, and Slavery: In the Crucible of Public Debate*. Chicago: University of Chicago Press, 1990.

Internet Sources

Home of the American Civil War, www.civilwarhome.com. This site is written by Civil War enthusiast and webmaster Dick Weeks. Updated weekly, the site provides pertinent information on events leading up to the Civil War and related topics on the Civil War era.

Smithsonian Institution, www.si.edu/resource/faq/nmah/civilwar.htm. This site offers an extensive bibliography of books related to Civil War history. It also provides a list of pertinent links to websites such as the U.S. Army Center for Military History and the U.S. Civil War Center.

Index